Cooking

with the

Texas Poets Laureate

Elizabeth Ethredge, Editor-in-Chief

**Editors: Joanna Baker, Matthew Bennett,
Reina Shay Broussard, Gary Horton,
and Julian Kindred**

Texas Review Press
Huntsville, Texas

FIRST EDITION, 2014
Requests for permission to reproduce material from this work should be sent to:
    Permissions
    Texas Review Press
    English Department
    Sam Houston State University
    Huntsville, TX 77341-2146

Cover photos courtesy of Chargriller and HEMISPHERES, a World of Fine Furnishings

Cover Design by Matt Bennett and Michael Ethredge

Poet Laureate Seal Desgin by Nancy Parsons

Wine Glass: Image courtesy of digitalart / FreeDigitalPhotos.net

Blue Crab: Image courtesy of antpkr / FreeDigitalPhotos.net

Honeycomb: Image courtesy of satit_srihin / FreeDigitalPhotos.net

Dirty Plates: Image courtesy of koratmember / FreeDigitalPhotos.net

Lime on a Tree: Image courtesy of anankkml / FreeDigitalPhotos.net

Strawberry Vine: Image courtesy of pixgood.com

Library of Congress Cataloging-in-Publication Data

Cooking with the Texas poets laureate / Elizabeth Ethredge, editor-in-chief ; editors:
Joanna Baker, Matthew Bennett, Reina Shay Broussard, Gary Horton, and Julian Kindred.
    pages cm
Summary: Contains recipes and food-related poetry and prose along with biographical
sketches of recent Texas poets laureate.
ISBN 978-1-68003-020-4 (pbk. : alk. paper)
1. Cooking--Texas. 2. Cooking, American--Poetry. 3. Poets laureate--Texas--Biography.
4. American poetry--21st century. I. Ethredge, Elizabeth, 1960- editor. II. Baker, Joanna,
1988- editor.
TX715.C78474 2014
641.59764--dc23

                            2014033032

In memory of Stephen Fromholtz (1945-2014)

and Carl Seale (1936-2014)

Dedicated to former and future Texas Poets Laureate,

for their inspiring and courageous artistic endeavors

from whom Texans learn new depths of enjoyment

and understanding in the human experience

History
of
Texas Poet Laureate

       In 1932, the government of Texas decided that, by golly, ten-gallon hats and cowboy boots just ain't cultural enough, so they threw together a committee to select a poet laureate, someone whose word-smithing was both exemplary, and easy enough for a cowboy to parse through. Their first selection was one Judd Mortimer Lewis from the great city of Houston, chosen by the governor of Texas, three senators, and three representatives under the authority of the 82nd Senate concurrent with the 43rd Legislature, which is an awfully long-winded way of sayin' the government of Texas made an executive decision to push the job off onto a small committee of big-shots.

       At first, a poet laureate was selected once every two years, but in 1961, the committee up and decided that if every two years was pretty darn good, every year would be even better, and that course was held until the 1990s. The nineties were a dark decade for poets with dreams of becoming the state's next laureate; only a single poet was singled out as worthy of the title-in 1992, one Mildred Baas of Victoria. But in a pique of wisdom, or perhaps some form of the millennium bug, the turn of the century brought with it a return to tradition, and a poet laureate has been selected every year since.

       And it just so happens that these remarkable men and women ain't just poets, but pretty darn good cooks, too . . . .

TABLE OF CONTENTS

2000 Texas Poet Laureate

STATE ARTIST AWARD

JAMES HOGGARD

WICHITA FALLS

POET'S BIO

James Hoggard, a teacher at Midwestern State University since 1966, has won numerous awards for his writing, including a National Endowment for the Arts Creative Writing Fellowship, the Soeurette Diehl Fraser Award for literary translation, the Brazos Bookstore (Houston) Award for the short story, and the Stanley Walker Award for the best newspaper journalism of the year by a writer from Texas. In addition, he was named a finalist in 1999 for the National Poetry Series Award.

His books include six collections of poems—most recently *Medea In Taos & Other Poems*(Pecan Grove) and *Rain In A Sunlit Sky* (Page One)—six collections of literary translations, a novel, a biography, and a collection of stories. His novel *Trotter Ross* was hailed by Leonard Randolph, the former director of literature for the NEA, as "far and away the finest masculine 'coming of age' novel in current American literature . . . a brilliant writer." His collection of stories, *Riding The Wind & Other Tales*, has been called "one of the finest books ever written by a Texas writer" (Dave Oliphant, *Texas Books in Review*). A dramatist as well as poet, fiction writer, and translator, he has had seven of his plays produced, including two in New York.

In addition to appearing in textbooks and anthologies, hundreds of his poems, stories, essays, and translations have appeared in such magazines and journals as *Southwest Review, Texas Monthly, The Texas Observer, Partisan Review, Redbook, Mississippi Review, Manoa, Ohio Review, Translation Review, Southern Living, Texas Parks & Wildlife, Dallas Morning News, Dallas Times Herald, Fort Worth Star-Telegram*, and numerous others.

2

DINNER AGAIN AT THEIR HOUSE

Beginning to end
the meal was well-spiced,
like the finely shifting
ranges of talk,
then early in the evening,
before we sat down,
my wife brought out
a platter full of armadillo eggs,
which most had never had before,
but most had also never had
her first choice, too:
squirrel jambalaya,
and understandably clear
was the fact I'd given up hunting
decades before, and the only gun
I had—a dead-eye single shot—
had a broken firing pin,
but all appeared to agree
we had a splendid range of tastes
that amplified
the deep-fried turkey,
the candied yams
and green chili cornbread
which was now on its way
to the table

How to Make Coq Au Vin

First wash the chicken—birds and people
have touched it before you,
you don't know where they've been

Now section the flesh, lay the pieces
in a pot—I prefer a narrow one—
juices do best when they rise high,
and you want the soak to go deep,
as far up into the meat as it can

Now quarter three onions and slide them
down in the pot with circles of carrots
and bite-sized chunks of potato

Next add a cup and a half of wine—
Burgundy's best—you want your meat
ripe-bodied and sharp—
most often that's what you want

I needn't prescribe the condiments here,
the amounts of garlic and salt to use,
or pepper and basil and thyme—
spices are a lot like love—

so cook the mix slowly, at not much more

than a simmer—the mix needs to steep,
needs to be in heat all day

Think of yourself with someone you love,
think of you both in bed all day,
the wrap and the press of your flesh
blushing your skin with its heat
By night you'll be ready to eat

Editor's Rendition

INGREDIENTS

- 2 boneless chicken breasts
- 3 boneless chicken thighs
- 4 strips bacon
- 1 medium onion, chopped
- 8 medium red potatoes quartered
- 3 carrots, sliced
- 1 ½ c each red wine (burgundy) and chicken broth
- 1 c mushrooms quartered

Spice Mixture

- 1 tsp kosher salt
- ½ tsp white pepper
- 1tsp each
    - basil, sage, thyme leaves
- ½ tsp celery salt
- 2 bay leaves

Preparation

Fry bacon in small crumbly pieces. Drain reserving grease. Wash chicken and pat dry, leaving whole. Season with salt and pepper. Brown chicken in bacon grease on both sides. Remove and set aside. After cooled, cut into pieces.

Large Crock Pot Version: Place browned chicken pieces, potatoes, and carrots in pot. In bacon grease, give a short sauté to mushrooms and onions, add remaining spices and liquid. Stir, then pour over chicken. Cook on low for 6-8 hours or high for 3-4. Garnish with crumbled bacon.

Oven version: In same pan, lightly sauté onions and mushrooms. Add potatoes and carrots, and spices. Place chicken in deep baking dish or Dutch oven. Cover with vegetables and add liquid. Cover with foil and bake at 350 degrees for 3 hours. Check at halfway point for liquid. Add ½ c of wine if needed. Remove foil and and add crumbled bacon. Finish baking.

WILD HONEY

We'd get our honey from the old dead tree,
night's chill helping us rush
when we disturbed the bees
by torching the buzzing trunk

We'd flail the swarm away
and rushing to the pond we'd heave
in the beam to stun the bees that stayed,
and we only got a few stings

Then hauling the trunk back out
we balanced it in our grip
and with it we ran through the dark
a mile or more to the house

Char and bees slopped on us like moss,
we reached the yard's penumbral light,
and cracking the trunk we snatched
hunks of comb free from the wood

The sticky cells were smoky,
sweetly gamy on the tongue

NOTES

2001 Texas Poet Laureate

STATE ARTIST AWARD

WALTER
MCDONALD

LUBBOCK

POET'S BIO

A Lubbock native, Walt is a retired U.S. Air Force pilot and retired from Texas Tech University as Paul W. Horn Professor of English Emeritus. With B.A. and M.A. degrees from Texas Tech and a Ph.D. from the University of Iowa, he taught for three tours of duty at the Air Force Academy and served in Vietnam.

Walt came to poetry late, as a middle-aged Air Force pilot during and after Vietnam. His 22 collections of poems and one book of short stories were published from 1976-2005. Four of his books won Western Heritage Awards from the National Cowboy Hall of Fame.

In 1987 Walt was appointed as a Paul Whitfield Horn Professor, Texas Tech's highest academic honor, named in memory of Tech's first President. Walt also received the Texas Professor of the Year Award in 1992 from CASE (the national Council for Advancement and Support of Education), and other awards from Texas Tech, including the Distinguished Alumnus Award, the President's Excellence in Teaching Award, the Distinguished Research Award, the President's Academic Achievement Award—and lifetime awards for writing from the Texas Book Festival and the Texas Institute of Letters. In 2001, the Texas House and Senate selected Walt as the 2001 Texas Poet Laureate.

By far his favorite award is their anniversary every August—for Carol and Walt were classmates at Lubbock High, and at the start of their sophomore year he told a friend, "I'm gonna marry that girl someday"—an audacious dream that came true.

THE NIGHT OF RATTLESNAKE CHILI

Only the lure of a rattler kept us
jerking dry tumbleweeds back
from the bunkhouse. Already, cook had
chili boiling, peppers and beef
convincing us all we were starving.

Cursing, throwing empty bean cans
at our horses, cook swore he'd douse
the fire and dump our dinner to the mules
unless we brought him a long dry tail
of rattler. I had heard of cooks

crazy enough to grind rattles
like chili powder, a secret poison
to make a pot boil darker than whiskey.
Kicking and calling each other names,
we scoured the yard for an hour,

a ranch so cursed with snakes
jackrabbits weren't safe while mating.
At last, I grabbed one by the tail,
the writhing muscle trying to escape
down a burrow, and Billy Ray shot it.

Cook cut off the tail and grinned,
held up the ticking rattle, then
crushed and ground it in his hands.
Hulls floated down into red steam,
and simmered. That night, we ate

thick chili redder than fire
and griped about the dust and hulls,
but begged for seconds. Even our beer
was cold and sweeter than most
and steel spoons melted in our mouths.

ONE MORNING BETWEEN WARS

The girl in the purple robe
tangled like a bath towel
lolls on the couch and laughs,
some pre-school song or clown trick
bouncing in her mind. Will she

years from now recall this Sunday morning
on the coast, up before Mommy
and her brothers, the lazy, purring world
all to herself? Will she remember
this hour of lounging, twisting

turning, and humming, her daddy
bringing breakfast on a tray,
the brittle bacon, the tiny tub of syrup,
hot strips of sweet French toast?
Will she miss the months he wasn't home,

the TV chant of *Desert Storm*
that grownups found exciting? He's back,
and now she lolls and rolls the bacon
on her lips, and nibbles, dips the toast
and dribbles sticky syrup on her tongue.

Her own real daddy brings
more bacon strips. He says she makes him
happy when she eats so well. Twisting
bacon like a rotor blade, she sings
about her daddy days ago, descending

from the sky like Santa Claus,
leaves blowing everywhere,
the whole crowd waving at her daddy's
helicopter, a real, brave daddy
finally back. She sniffs the bacon,

lips it, sucks it like a lollypop
and hums, God up in heaven,
her daddy close enough to hear her
when she calls, another strip
of French toast in her bowl.

Walt McDonald as a USAF pilot.

Sugar-less Banana Nut Cake

Ingredients

- 1 c safflower oil
- 1 c Splenda Sugar Blend
- 2 eggs, well beaten
- 5 very ripe bananas, mashed
- 2 $\frac{1}{3}$ c flour
- 1 tsp salt
- 2 tsp soda dissolved in 4 Tbsp hot water
- 1 Tbsp vanilla
- 1 c pecans broken into pieces

Cream Cheese Frosting

- 2 8-oz pkgs Cream Cheese (use $\frac{1}{3}$ less fat, if preferred)
- ½ c Splenda Sugar Blend
- 1 stick soften butter
- 1 tsp vanilla
- dab of Half-n-Half if needed

Preparation

Pre-heat oven at 325 degrees. Mix in order given. Pour into well-greased and floured 9x13 pan. Bake for 25 minutes in pre-heated oven at 325 degrees or until toothpick test is clean. Remove from oven allow to completely cool before frosting.

Editor's note: Substituting with anything other than Splenda Sugar Blend might not taste the same.

ROCKET ATTACK

Crack like a screen door slammed
and cannon fire. After that first explosion,
silence, then fallout that clattered down.
I heard shouts and sirens and saw men run,

the roar of choppers and gunfire at dawn,
the rumble of bombs. I remember the weird
thrill of falling hard as they taught,
someone throwing up next door in fear.

I remember waking later, stunned that I slept
after that. I followed echoes in my skull
to the shattered hooch, airmen dead
in a crater fifty feet east—their blood

splattered like motor oil. MP's stood guard,
and corpsmen sifted smoking dirt for bones
or flesh. I remember breakfast was lard
and runny eggs with ketchup and burned toast

butter-soaked, and bacon fried soggy
in a tent reeking of greasy smoke and wood.
It seemed insane—but the fragile body
was hungry, *and it was good, it tasted good.*

Dogbread Recipe:
Traditional Family Recipe

"A little like cornbread, but without eggs & baking powder. For folks, but dogs like it, too."

Ingredients

1½ c cornmeal (yellow or white)
½ c flour (more or less, for different texture and taste)
1 tsp salt
$^{1}/_{3}$ c Crisco
2 c boiling water

Preparations

Heat oven to 450 degrees. Grease a cookie sheet (rectangular) and heat in oven until Crisco melts. Carefully remove from oven. In a mixing bowl, combine cornmeal, flour, and salt. Add the lump of Crisco and cut into the dry mixture until it's coarsely mixed. Stir in 1 cup boiling water, mixing until dry ingredients are moistened. Add more boiling water, if needed, until you can pick up a ball of the batter in your hands. With wet hands, divide the batter into about twelve balls. Place on cookie sheet, four down and three across. Wet hands again, and mash each ball down with knuckles—to make ½ inch thick pones. (These will not spread out when baking.) Bake for about 25 minutes—or until the ridges are light-to-golden brown.

If we're in a hurry—or sometimes just for variety—Carol places the batter balls in a greased large skillet or griddle, mashes them down and cooks them on the stove. It's faster, and they look and even taste different from the oven-cooked ones we prefer.

We like this with any kind of beans, black-eyed peas, greens, homemade vegetable or vegetable-beef soup—or only dogbread with onions! Carol likes a dab of butter melting. Enjoy!

Editor Note: Pictured with Frijoles Borrachos, a Jan Seale recipe.

Cayenne Cheese Patties

Ingredients

   1 stick butter

   1 jar Old English cheese

   1 c flour

   1 c Rice Krispies

   ¼ tsp cayenne pepper

   ½ tsp salt

Preparation

Heat oven to 425 degrees. Mix butter and Old English cheese. Add 1 cup flour with the salt and cayenne pepper. Mix well. Fold in Rice Krispies. Make into balls and flatten with fork. Bake for 8 to10 minutes at 425 degrees. Transfer to a cooling rack.

NOTES

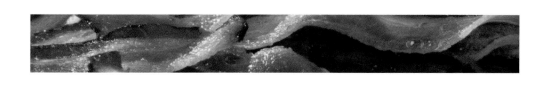

2004 Texas Poet Laureate

STATE ARTIST AWARD

CLEATUS RATTAN

CISCO

Poet's Bio

Cleatus Rattan attended seven universities and earned five degrees from four of them: Southern Methodist University, the University of North Texas (two degrees), Hardin Simmons University, and Texas A&M University-Commerce. Rattan claims not to be well educated, but he was, he said, *frequently* educated.

More importantly, Rattan was selected as Most Handsome Boy at Irving High School in 1951 and 1952. He was not nominated for this distinction in his senior year. Bushism in Florida, he suspects. Rattan played the part of Nanki Poo in the immortal Irving High School production of *The Mikado* in 1952, and some say the strains of "A Wandering Minstrel, I" continue to waft through the old non-venerated building. In addition, he was chosen by his senior teammates as The Man Most Likely to Hit the Ball Carrier After He Was Down. His eyes always grow moist at the thought of such an honor.

Rattan's greatest honor was being selected as husband to the former Connie Hood of Borger, Texas, in 1961, a school beauty for each of the three years she required to earn a degree in music from the University of North Texas. Although Mrs. Rattan, the elder (as distinguished from her daughters-in-law), earned no degree higher than the MA, her husband and sons continue to adore her despite her lack of formal education. She increased the honor to her husband by presenting him with three perfect sons: Randall Hampton Rattan, PhD; Jason Cleatus Rattan, DVM; and Raiford Adrian Rattan, MD. All the brothers are valiant.

Dr. Cleatus Rattan gave commencement addresses at Texas A&M University-Commerce and the University of North Texas, where he emphasized getting to work on time, staying sober, the value of marriage, along with other intellectual advice.

BIG WORDS, PASTRIES

Just before a final exam in Greek Literature.
I hurriedly purchased a cream-filled pastry
from the Amore Shop in the plaza.
Hurrying to the exam, I slipped
it into my coat pocket. At my graffiti-profaned desk,
with my coat across my lap, I caressed my pastry,
surreptitiously extracting it
when Helen joyously, gamine-like, plopped on my lap.

(A sensible man would have hung
the coat on the back of the chair, I know.
Strange what Athena, Aphrodite have us do.)

Helen felt something without doubt
odd, looked on
my mess-filled lap,
massaged her creamy butt,
misapprehended,
hurled angry imprecations at the sky.

Such words are always punished, frequently ridiculed.

For the next two years, she kept
her silence. Ten years distant
in a downward elevator
in the Worthington, we were together
with our mates. Oh the Fates!
I spoke. She did not. She turned away
like Dido. You must admire a world-class grudge.
I have contacted Guinness.

Hera taught her.

To her address, listed in the alumni bulletin,
I have mailed a box of gooey pastries
every May since that elevator meeting ten years past.
I sign "Messmaker" on a slightly altered reproduction
of Thetis with her hands on Zeus' knees,
seemingly horrified.

Bacon and Lots of Stuff

This is a dish that should be served with a defibrillator. And do not eat this a week before a blood test. This is an old East Texas dish my grandmother made to serve about twelve people, but you may increase or use less of the ingredients. Nothing precise about how much is to be used, but use variations of ingredients all made to taste.

Probably need to try this one a few times. I only guess as to how much of what. My grandmother would not be pinned down as to how much of any ingredient any closer than "large or small spoons full" and "pinches" of various things. She lived to be 91, but had she not eaten this dish, she might still be alive, and she died in 1975. The thing seems like a casserole to me. Brunchy stuff! A family favorite.

Ingredients

About 8 slices of peppered bacon cut into about 1 inch pieces
1 red bell pepper, sliced thinly (or not)
2 c of white mushrooms, also sliced
2 cloves garlic, thinly sliced
6-8 large eggs
2-2½ c whole milk
½ c cream
½ c of thinly sliced chives
1 Tbsp* each of chopped oregano, rosemary, & thyme
salt (you decide how much salt, but it can be overdone—maybe ½ tsp or so)
ground black pepper (I usually use a full tsp or slightly more)
a loaf of French bread (must be fresh) cut into thin slices (half inch or so, err on the side of thinner)
2 c shredded cheese

PREPARATION

Cook the thing in a large frying pan (East Texas talk). You may use a skillet, as we say in West Texas, at medium heat about 6 to 10 minutes. Bacon should be crisp, but inch-sized bacon becomes crisp pretty quick. "Pretty quick" is a technical term, I know. Put bacon on several paper towels and save the bacon fat in frying pan. In that same pan cook the bell peppers, garlic, and mushrooms about 3 or 4 minutes or until it all begins to brown. Stir in the bacon and quit cooking.

Spray a deep dish with that kind of spray, the name of which eludes me. In a large bowl beat in (I think that is the term) eggs, milk, cream, salt, pepper, herbs. Use about half of the ingredients to make a first layer. Put bread slices on the bottom. Distribute all the stuff evenly—all the bacon, pepper, mushrooms—over the bread and sprinkle in the shredded cheese. Repeat with all the remaining ingredients, finishing with all the remaining egg mixture. Cover the dish and refrigerate for an hour, or as I usually do, leave the thing in the fridge overnight.

Preheat the oven to 350 (ain't that always the number?), and bake for about 45 minutes or until the egg is set and the top is starting to brown and bubble. Let it stand for a while and serve. Invite a physician to your dinner, and check your will.

BACON BLOODY MARY

J & D's Bacon Salt is available online or at specialty food stores. If necessary, bacon flavored vodka such as Bakon can be specially ordered at your liquor store. For approximately 4 glasses of 8 ounces use:

INGREDIENTS

2 Tbsp Worcestershire sauce
2 Tbsp freshly squeezed lemon juice
1 tsp horseradish
½ tsp Tabasco sauce
¼ tsp celery seed
¼ tsp ground coriander
¼ tsp ground black pepper
¼ tsp salt
20 oz tomato juice
6-8 oz (or to taste) vodka
   recommend bacon flavored vodka
2 Tbsp Bacon Salt
lime wedges

PREPARATION

Pour all of the above into a large pitcher except tomato juice and vodka. Then add the tomato juice and vodka. Stir well and refrigerate. Garnish each glass with a bacon twist. Rub the rim of each glass with the lime wedge. Then dip glasses in the bacon salt.

For bacon swizzle sticks, if desired, use 4 to 8 slices of thinly cut bacon, and wrap the bacon slices around disposable chopsticks in a spiral. Place the chopsticks on a foil-lined baking sheet. Bake until the bacon becomes brown and crispy—15 to 20 minutes in a preheated oven at 425 degrees.

Cool completely before gently removing the chopsticks from the bacon.

Green Chile Chicken Enchiladas

This is a dish my wife of 53 years brought into our marriage as part of her trousseau (however one spells that word).

Ingredients

12 corn tortillas
3 Tbsp flour
½ c salad oil (for frying tortillas)
2 c chicken broth
2 c grated Monterey Jack Cheese

1 c sour cream
¾ c chopped onion
2 c diced boned chicken
¼ c butter
1 can (4 oz) chopped green chiles

Preparation

In a frying pan (okay, skillet), cook tortillas 5 seconds on each side to soften them. Place 2 tablespoons of cheese and 1 tablespoon of onion on each tortilla and roll up. Place seam side down in baking dish. Melt butter in a large skillet and blend in flour. Add broth and cook until thick. Stir in sour cream, chicken, and chiles. Cook until heated, but do not boil. Pour over tortillas. Sprinkle with remaining cheese. Bake at 350 for 30 minutes.

I suppose I should add that one of my three sons is a physician, and he eats all these things, but another son is a veterinarian and a vegan, and he says he has to live a long life for his daughter's sake, so he will not eat all this cheese. I am sure he is correct, but with all this fracking, foul water, global warming, among asteroids and many other problems for this cancer growth of overpopulating of our tender planet, don't sweat the small stuff.

Editor Note: The heat is in the chilies. Use hotter chilles to preference. Chicken used was grilled on a BBQ pit a day before. Also good with cheddar cheese. Tortillas were heated without the oil on a non-stick griddle and were great, very easy to roll.

A Memoir

When I was a young man, I left SMU without taking a degree (until many years later). I joined the Marine Corps, a sort of an attempt at suicide that came too near coming true all too often. After three years in the Corps, I had risen to the illustrious rank of Sergeant, and I was offered the opportunity of Officers Candidate School, known in the Corps as OTC, not OCS as in the army. The OTC was a three-month process, but the following nine-months was a much more difficult time known as Basic School. Consequently, I had only seen a TV set one day during that year, and that was to watch Texas play Texas A&M on Thanksgiving Day.

When I was at SMU, I dated a girl from my hometown whom I had ogled in high school. She graduated from SMUUU-land and began to teach at a grade school in Dallas. As I was on my way overseas, I received a package from her that held about 30 letters to me from her third-grade class. I remember being thought of as an odd sort when I opened that large envelope. However, after a year of teaching, she quit and took a job as a stewardess, as they were known in those days, for American Airlines.

When I returned to the U. S. and after receiving my commission, I was assigned to the 3rd Battalion of the 5th Marine Regiment of the 1st Marine Division, where I was told by a colonel with ribbons up to his ear that the most obnoxious persons on earth were Marine 2nd Lieutenants who had graduated from Texas A&M. I hastily told him I had been at SMU. He said it made no difference.

At any rate, my girlfriend from my hometown and SMU arranged to take flights from Dallas to San Diego one weekend and then to LAX on the following weekends. I would pick her up at either airport for weekends at my apartment at Oceanside, California, which is about 30 miles north of San Diego and about 70 miles south of Los Angeles.

One Friday afternoon, I arrived at the El Cajon hotel, a plush place at that time, to pick up my girlfriend. (I'll call her Nancy because that was and still is her name.) As I was standing close to the front desk using the house phone to call her, I noticed a certain electricity in the room. A dark haired, muscular man in a blue Banlon shirt with a little alligator on the left breast pocket, to whom everyone was being obsequious, had come to the desk, followed by a small, equally dark-haired bellboy carrying the heaviest bag of golf clubs I had ever seen. Everyone was referring to the man as Mr. Maverick. While I was overseas dealing with some unfriendly natives and sparring with the unfriendly instructors at OTC and Basic School, he, an ex-marine I later learned, had become famous for playing the part of Brett Maverick on the tube.

I went upstairs to Nancy's room—a room she shared with another stewardess—to tell her of Mr. Maverick with wonder in my voice as to who he was. She became excited, dressed hurriedly to see him for herself, but alas as we arrived he had just gone up to his room, we were told. My deflated Nancy and I went out to dinner, where she told me a great deal more about him than I was interested in knowing. I wanted to bask in being an officer and had prepared to tell her of all my glories. She was not interested. She wanted Mr. Maverick.

Later that night we returned to the hotel and stopped at the bar for one last drink. When we walked into the bar, we saw Mr. Maverick at the bar. We, too, sat at the bar, though it would have been improper for a lady to sit at the bar in Dallas, the custom, in California, was perfectly acceptable. Only slightly shocked at the change in culture, she wanted to see him in the mirror, and she did. She stared; I hid quick glances, she just stared. In a few minutes the bellboy came into the bar followed by my girlfriend's roommate. They walked in tandem to a spot directly behind Mr. Maverick, where the bellboy said, "Mr. Maverick, Gloria here would like to meet you." Mr. Maverick slowly rolled around on his bar stool and looked at Gloria up and down, and then again up and down, then turned around on his stool and continued looking at himself in the mirror. He had said not a word. I remember the scream from Gloria and her high heels hitting the marble floor as she ran out of the room. The bellboy, almost equally embarrassed, slinked out after her, though not as quickly. The three other couples in the room, all in booths, and Nancy and I were saddened and thoroughly depressed to have witnessed that scene.

The next day at the pool, Mr. Maverick, with another beauty at his side, arrived at the pool. I thought for a few minutes, walked about three steps up to him, and politely told him that he had been unforgivably rude. He looked surprised and said he didn't remember that moment. I didn't believe him and told him so. We talked, and then we talked some more. He offered an apology that sounded sincere and told me some of his Marine experiences. Hard to believe, but before the morning was over, we had become friends. He said he could call Gloria and apologize, but as he was with another lady, that call was about all he could do. I agreed to convey his apology.

He and his friend were headed back to LA, and I surprised myself by asking him to stop by my apartment, where I could cook a bacon-wrapped sirloin that would be better than he could find in LA. As it turned out, we all stayed another day in San Diego and hit some spots that I would have never been able to get in, I'm sure. I bragged, however, that I was a better chef with some dishes than the ones he knew. On Sunday, he surprised me by saying he was waiting to taste my concoction. We headed in tandem to Oceanside, where I cooked for him. He stayed a while, we took a swim in the Pacific and had a few drinks, and he left for LA after giving me his phone number, telling me I was a better cook than some he knew in LA. I didn't tell him that my cuisine menu was limited. But this is not the end of the story.

Last year, as I was visiting my second son in LA, where he is a doctor, we went to Nate 'n Al's in Beverly Hills for breakfast. The deli is well known for harboring luminaries. Larry King, with Mike Shapiro, the attorney who became famous during the O.J. trial, has breakfast there seven days a week. (I continue to sneak peeks at all luminaries.)

On the day when we went there (my wife and I go to LA often), James Garner walked in. He was fat, bald, and leaning on a walker, rolling it along. I took a minute or two to recognize him, and he stared back at me, obviously puzzled as to who I was. As he was leaving, he continued to stare at me, so I walked over to him (he was easy to catch) and introduced myself. After some jolting moments when I was thinking I had just made an ass of myself, he finally remembered our weekend and laughed. He then came back to my table and met my wife, son, and daughter-in-law and told them much more of that weekend than I wanted him to. My daughter-in-law, I am pleased to say, was impressed, as I suspect were all the other patrons of the famous deli. Oh, I asked him if he remembered my cooking, and he said no. Shucks, if you will forgive my language.

Love, Cleatus

Bacon-Wrapped Beef Tenderloins with Pomegranate Glaze

INGREDIENTS
>   4 beef tenderloin steaks (4-6 oz each)
>   salt and coarsely ground pepper
>   4 slices thick-cut, peppered bacon
>   2 Tbsp olive oil (less if using nonstick skillet)

PREPARATION

Preheat oven to 450. Sprinkle each steak generously with salt and pepper. Wrap each steak with one slice of thick-cut bacon, securing the ends with toothpicks.

Heat the olive oil in a large skillet, preferable cast iron, over high heat. Sear the steaks to a nice brown, about 2 minutes on each side, using tongs to carefully roll the steaks on their sides to quickly sear the bacon all the way around. Transfer the skillet to the oven and cook, flipping the steaks once halfway through the cooking until the steaks are done to your liking and the bacon is cooked. About 10 minutes for medium. Remove and discard the toothpicks, unless you want a souvenir. Serve the steaks hot, drizzled with pomegranate glaze. Serves 4.

POMEGRANATE GLAZE
INGREDIENTS
>   1 c pomegranate juice
>   ½ c balsamic vinegar
>   ¼ c light brown sugar
>   4 tsp chopped fresh rosemary (2 long twigs)ww
>   salt

PREPARATION

Combine the pomegranate juice, vinegar, sugar. Bring to a boil over high heat. Then simmer over medium heat until reduced by half, about 15 to18 minutes. Season to taste.

Something of a Memoir

When I was in the Marine Corps, I became interested in cooking. I was a 23-year-old 2nd Lieutenant who had just graduated from Officers Training School about six months before being assigned to an Admiral Emmit O'Beirne's staff as an aid. The admiral had asked for a Marine Lieutenant who spoke French. The Admiral was waiting to be sent to the Med when I joined his staff in Hong Kong. The Admiral always wanted an ex-enlisted Marine on his staff (I had been in the Corps for three years and three months before being sent to officer's training), largely because he thought we wore our uniforms well, and he wanted a Marine Officer to review Courts Martial of Marines. I had little to do, and all the others on the Admiral's staff were academy men who outranked me and for a while paid little attention to a Marine 2nd Lieutenant.

I had left SMU after my second year, and the only courses I had made A's in were French courses. I had an edge because my grandmother was a French woman who had married my grandfather when he was in France in 1918. My grandfather was a Marine, of course. My grandmother spoke French exclusively to me. She was determined that one of her grandchildren should speak French. I was the one she chose because we lived in the same little town as my grandparents. I thought it was fun to speak French because I imagined it appealed to the girls in my high school. Looking back, I think they were not overly interested. Shucks, if you will forgive my language.

I began to find something in common with the other staff members when we started to watch a British comedian whose name was, and may still be, Graham Kerr. I loved his jokes and detested Brit cooking. The base we were on was a Brit base, and the food was Brit. All of us on the staff came to like Chinese cooking, and as I remember we all disliked the Brit crap. Kerr's cooking was more to our taste, pun intended. One day (a day-time show) when we were learning and taking notes on his recipes for those on duty, Kerr told a joke that struck all of as odd and later we laughed at it for years. I continue to share recipes with some of those guys, and we usually make some remarks even today about what he made funny, though we were never sure why we laughed so hard. One example is one of the hundreds of three wishes jokes.

A genie appears on the isle of Malta to help with the racial problems. After a series of lectures punctuated with cooking stories and recipes, the genie offers the three reps of each ethnic group one wish each. The first person, a black man, expressed his wish to rid the isle of the whites and Asians. The wish was to be granted. The second wish was offered to an Asian who expressed his wish to rid the island of the Brits and the blacks. The genie looked puzzled, but he asked the Englishman for his wish and the Englishman said, "Could I have a pink gin, please?"

I still laugh, but I find many of my friends look blankly at me when I tell that joke. The recipe for that day was for Maple Bacon Frosting.

Love, Cleatus

34

Maple Bacon and Cream Cheese Frosting

INGREDIENTS
- 1 package (8 oz) cream cheese, softened
- ½ c (1 stick) unsalted butter, softened
- 2 Tbsp pure maple syrup
- 2 c powered sugar, sifted
- ¼ c chopped, toasted pecans
- ¼ c cooked and crumbled bacon—about 3 slices

PREPARATION

In an electric mixer, beat the cream cheese and butter on medium speed until smooth and evenly combined. Add the maple syrup. With mixer on low, gradually add the powdered sugar until the frosting is thick and spreadable. Fold in the toasted pecans and bacon bits.

Makes 3 cups to frost 12 cupcakes.

Picture Courtesy of the Galloping Gourmet, grahamkerr.com.

NOTES

ALAN
BIRKELBACH

PLANO

Poet's Bio

Alan Birkelbach, a native Texan, was the 2005 Poet Laureate of Texas. He grew up in central Texas on a wonderful mixed up diet of English food, German-church-event food, barbecue, Mexican dishes and pie. He wrote his first poem years before he met his first egg-roll. He's fascinated how people tend to tie food to events. He likes simple recipes—that have lots of flavor. His poetry work has appeared in journals and anthologies such as *Grasslands Review, Borderlands, The Langdon Review, and Concho River Review.* He has nine collections of poetry and is a member of the Academy of American Poets.

MENU

Bound in knots we had no idea our bodies could form
we twist the sheets past their normal boundaries,
our toes and knees snagging as we roll,
legs snarled on legs.

When we cooked Thanksgiving dinner
we had to restrict our menu. We did not recognize
any lines between appetizer, entrée,
and dessert. Bowl and pans and whisks

slowly spread from room to room,
each dish another incursion as it was mixed.
We had to be careful in the den not to sit on
roaming wooden spoons!

When we moved in it didn't take a week for us
to roll outside the confines of the bedroom
and christen the hallway, the stairs, the backyard,
the kitchen,

letting the anticipated flavor of something new
guide our stirrings and frothings. Hmmm.
Something smells good. My mouth is watering.
How shall we feast today? And where?

FLAMING LOVE

I stand by my theory that just about all men of my generation, and probably my father's generation too, believed that they could do three things better than any other man in the world, including the man they were standing next to, be it brother or uncle. Those three things were: playing pool, imitating Elvis, and grilling meat. I don't think these lessons were explicitly taught, I certainly don't remember any sit-down sessions, yet all of my male peers seemed to know (in theory) exactly where to strike the cue ball to make the other clustered balls explode on a break, they all seemed to know exactly how to move their hips and sneer like Elvis (which they would gladly show you if no women were around), and they all seemed to have a genetically-imprinted professional opinion about how they could grill the steaks or chicken even better than the bare-sleeved fifty-gallon-drum-pit-boss currently in charge.

I will admit that I did have a certain envy for those guys who seemed to have the eye for playing pool. They knew the steps of the dance around the green felt tables; they fulfilled the image of the loner, cigarettes hanging from their lips while they eyed along the cue, their half-empty Lone Star bottle waiting for them on the nearby round, green formica table.

And the Elvis thing, well, while the moves were handy, it required a certain amount of courage to do them in public to impress a girl because if one guy did it then you had to be willing to step up and out-do that guy. It could be a tiny, rockabilly chain reaction: one guy would start—and then the whole shimmy thing would travel down the line, all the participants hoping a cluster of nearby girls might pay attention. It was truly a crowing-rooster type of dynamic. If you had a leather jacket and black hair, I think you got extra points.

But the grilling thing: this was different. It wasn't necessarily a display/sexual bravado dynamic. It was even more primal than that. Every man had his theory about how long to cook the meats (whatever they were), what type of wood to use, how to test for done-ness—and so on. (And here I have to say I am not venturing into the discussion about barbecue, the most holy of meat cooking. Grilling and barbecuing are not the same. No sir.) Why, even the youngest of male children had an opinion (although theirs was generally limited as to whether they preferred char or no char on their hot dogs and how they could have, and had, done it better. Probably at church camp.)

Of course, grilling, like the other two firm-held beliefs, was a false parable. At least, in my experience it was. By the time I was fifteen I learned that I could no longer harbor any illusions about my pool playing ability. I will only say that it is crushing to be pre-pubescent and have it soundly pointed out to you that you do not have a pool-playing ability that obviously all the other boys your age, and probably also their younger brothers, have.

The Elvis gyrating, well, more on that later.

Let's talking about cooking for a while. When I was growing up, my father would periodically host informal cookouts in our backyard. He would call them barbecues, and certainly a ketchup-based sauce was involved, but really it was grilling. Generally he would start a coal-bed in a split-horizontal, modified fifty-gallon drum, let the fire burn down, then throw oak or pecan limbs on the conflagration, and keep a low-level flame going. The meat was usually rabbit or chicken, lots of chicken. Hot dogs and hamburgers. Nothing cooked or smoked long-term. We weren't wealthy enough for steaks. But there was chicken. Lots of chicken.

He was really good at it. He truly did have that sense of how to cook on a grill. The meat was always done exactly right, just barely smoky but still juicy and flavorable. Hamburgers were always done, just past pink. Hot dogs—it was like they were ready to jump barking and fully-cooked into a bun. He had it down—and even when I was little I admired that skill level. I instinctively knew two things: that he was a better griller than any other man—and that I would never be so good.

Even after he retired, and my sisters and I moved away, he continued to enjoy cooking on the grill. When we would stop by to visit, he would sometimes throw hot dogs or hamburgers on the grill and serve us up some memories.

But cooking, and especially grilling, is a skill. And like most other skills they can erode. Unlike some skills, where you have to keep practicing to keep the edge up, sometimes the skill seems to have a mind of its own—and just up and starts packing its bags. It isn't tied to dementia or old age or anything like that. One day you can make a legendary margarita and the next day you can't. That's what happened to my dad.

I knew everything was done for him one day when we stopped by and he grilled us some hamburgers. He seemed to have such faith in his abilities that he could walk away from the grill and do something else. Almost like Jesus would man the tongs. Any self-respecting griller knows you cannot walk away. You need to stay around. On this particular epiphanous day—he did not stay around. And when we did have dinner later, most of us tried to politely conversationally rationalize how the hunks of charcoal tasted just fine, thank you. In reality, the meal was a chorus of bituminous crunching.

I knew that day I wanted to reject that genetic predisposition. So, I went in a different direction: using a smoker. I will not preach here on the glory that is cooking in a smoker. I will say now that it does appeal to me on a level easily associated with my previous story: I can start the fire, put the meat on, and walk away. In my version Jesus can walk away too. At least for a couple of hours.

I won't go into detail much here about the mechanics of cooking meat on a smoker. You need to learn your own self about how to start the fire, how long to soak the wood. I will say this: This is less about the smoker you use than how you do it. I use a Brinkman's smoker. It's about three feet tall and looks like a little torpedo and costs about $40. It has a fire pan, a water pan, and two meat racks. I have two other smokers, different dynamics set-up wise, and they both produce excellent meals. I will add: for this recipe I like to smoke over mesquite wood. With a little pecan wood (pecan shells are okay) thrown in if I can get it. This recipe is for Baby Back Ribs.

Baby Back Ribs

1st Step: Buy two racks of Baby Back ribs and a roll of aluminum foil, one
        to line the charcoal pan in the smoker, the other to wrap the ribs in rub
        overnight
2nd Step: Prepare Rib Rub.
3rd Step: Cook ribs.

Here's the rib rub recipe. A good rib rub makes all the difference. A bad rub
cooked over good wood will not result in good ribs. But a good rub, over just
plain old oak—yeah, it will work just fine.

Rib Rub Recipe

INGREDIENTS
    ¼ c paprika
    2 Tbsp sea salt (you can use plain salt)
    2 Tbsp onion powder
    2 Tbsp garlic powder
    2 Tbsp ground black pepper
    1 Tbsp white pepper
    1 Tbsp cayenne
    ¾ c brown sugar

Generally, you can add a little plain white sugar if you like—but cut back on
the brown sugar then. Some folks like to add rosemary or Italian seasoning.
Me—I just add more black pepper. Just add the items one at a time into a
large bowl. No special order. If you let the rub sit at least overnight, I think the
melding of flavors is better. This makes more than enough for two racks of ribs.
Put the rest in a sealable plastic tub. It keeps for weeks and weeks.

Preparation

Peel the membrane off the back of the ribs. (It's a thin layer of skin on the
back of the ribs. There is a thin layer and a thick layer. Start at the tip end of
the ribs. You'll find the start of it easily enough. Grab that membrane with
your fingernails and pull it off like old paint. It might take a few minutes. Don't
be neurotic about getting it all off. The thick layer is right underneath the thin
layer. If you take off the thick layer the ribs will fall apart too soon.)

Once you have peeled the ribs, then coat them in the rib rub, generously,
both sides. Set them on a large pan or cookie sheet. You can stack them.
Cover them in foil. Stick them in the fridge overnight. (You can let them sit just
a few hours if you like. The longer they sit—the better the flavor.)

Plan your wood a day ahead. Whatever wood you plan on using you should set aside about 15-20 pieces about half-fist size. That's your dry wood. Take the same amount and soak them in a bucket of water overnight. Next day, prepare the fire. (Do not use lighter fluid. It will stink up your charcoal and stink up your meat.) When you have the charcoal going, that is the time you add about 5 pieces of dry wood and 5 pieces of wet wood. I like a smoker with a water pan. That water pan holds about 2 quarts of water—and a beer. Some type of beer. I like Shiner Bock or a Porter or a Stout. Once you are sure the fire is ready, then put one rack of ribs on one metal grate, another on the other metal grate, shut the lid on the smoker, and walk away.

Check back in about half an hour to make sure the fire is at a good temp. (Most smoker have a temperature gauge that says something like LOW, IDEAL, or HOT. That IDEAL range is pretty-wide as temperatures go. 150-250 degrees is about ideal.)

After an hour go open the smoker, flip the ribs, check the coal-bed (add more wet or dry wood as necessary), add more water to the water pan if you need to, then walk away again. Another half hour or so.
In another half hour, open the smoker, switch the two racks (so the top ribs are now the bottom and vice versa), then close the smoker and walk away. Really, the trick to all this is keep the temperature in the IDEAL range.
Right at the two hour mark your ribs are ready. Two hours. It is an intoxicating, sweet-bitey flavor. Claim three ribs early. They go quickly.

Oh yeah. Back to Elvis. Trust me on this, guys. Less than a tenth of one percent of us truly knows how to do that hip swivel. Don't try it. If you try it past your fifties you will regret it. You cannot imitate Elvis. You have never been able to imitate Elvis. Or John Wayne either.

THAT'S AMORE
OR
IT'S NOT ABOUT THE LIRA

While people tend to be willing to attempt to cook all types of fancy salmon or sushi or cheesy-bacony-potato combos, I have talked to very few people who have been willing to attempt to make their own pizzas.

It's understandable. Pizza is ubiquitous. You can get it for $5, fully cooked, ready to eat. Pizza occupies at least two full vertical columns in the freezer at the grocery store. Pizza is a casual-go-out-to-eat meal—which is why nobody makes it at home. It isn't time- or cost-effective.

It's true that buying the ingredients you want on YOUR pizza will end up costing you more than if you just went and bought a franchise pizza. That's undeniable. But then you would miss out on some of the best olfactory experiences—not to mention incredible flavors—that can only be accomplished by doing it yourself.

And I might as well say up front: there is one thing you are almost certainly going to want to try and do—try to spin the dough in the air like you see in the commercials.

Go on. Go ahead and try it. You gotta do it. Good luck with that.

Ready? Okay.

On some occasions, not tied to a specific day, our family decides we will make homemade pizzas. Two people are put in charge of making enough dough. (That is usually me and one of my daughters.) The core tribe, when gathered, is fourteen people. Guests are always welcome and have to be accounted for in the dough planning. Also, my daughter and I tend to do at least 2, sometimes 3 different types of dough (plain, Italian herb, garlic, etc—sometimes even a sweet dough for a dessert pizza.)

Construction is usually an independent sport. But this type of cooking is good because it involves all parties. EVERYONE is in the kitchen making their own pizza. Everyone is involved in the celebration, regardless of whether it's a birthday or New Year's or Mother's Day. Doesn't matter. Everybody brings the toppings they want. Nothing is off the menu (as long as no one else has to eat it.) Just compare this with writing a poem—another independent sport. In this version everybody gets to submit a line. Or couplet. It's crazy. But it works.

There are some things you will absolutely need up front:

At least 1, if not 3 or 4, pizza stones (1 stone—1 pizza). How big is your crowd? I have a minimum of 4 going at once. As an aside, but it's important: there are two basic shapes of pizza stone: square or large round. The square is about the size of a household floor tile (about a foot square.) The round ones are usually about 15 inches across. If it's only kids you're cooking for then the small, square ones are fine. But for adults, go for the big round ones.) A pizza paddle (a long, wooden oar-like thing). You only need one of these. Generally you can get them at any home gadget store. You'll think you won't need it, that a spatula or an edgeless cookie sheet will do just fine. Trust me on this. You'll need it.

A rolling pin (reference the dough tossing hint earlier). Listen. Do you know how to spin a Frisbee on the end of your finger? If you do not—then use a rolling pin to flatten the dough.

    Hot oven mitts.
    Multiple trivets.
    A large, flat surface to roll dough on.
    A bag of corn meal. A cheap, small bag will do fine.
    At LEAST a five-pound bag of flour.
    At LEAST 2 3-pack strips of yeast. You can buy yeast in various forms. I use the yeast that comes in prepackaged strips.

Basic Pizza Dough Recipe

INGREDIENTS
    2 Tbsp sugar
    1 Tbsp salt (I like sea salt. It's got a different pop to it.)
    1½ Tbsp olive oil
    ¾ c warm water (plus 1 Tbsp of warm water to start the yeast)
    3-4 c flour (For pizza dough, I like bread flour. Regular flour is fine.
        Self-rising works great, too.)
    1 package instant yeast (1 package for EACH large ball of pizza dough)
    Tomato sauce (Generally 1 can will do multiple pizzas depending on how
        much of a sauce hog you are.)

PREPARATION
    Dissolve the yeast into about a tablespoon of barely warm water and set aside for a minimum of 10 minutes. Mix 2 cups of flour, sugar, salt, and the olive oil into a large non-metallic bowl. Add the ¾ cup warm water. Stir it all together. After the ten minutes have passed on the yeast then add it into this bowl. Stir it all together. It's okay to use your hands. A wooden spoon is okay too. (If you are going to add anything to the

dough, like Italian herbs, or garlic, or anything like that, now is the time to do it.)

The mix will probably be too wet and sticky. Add more flour, sparingly, until you have a smooth, non-tacky ball. You can either knead the dough there in the bowl or in the next step on the large, flat surface. (No, you don't have to knead it long. You basically want to break it up a little and make it elastic—and make sure it's not too dry or too wet.)

NOTE: If you have time, this is when you set the dough aside and let it rise. To do that, you leave the dough in the bowl, cover the whole thing with a kitchen towel, and leave it in a warm place. Don't put it in the fridge. A sunny spot on the table is best. Let it sit, undisturbed, about an hour. After an hour remove the towel and literally punch the dough down then knead it a little more. If you don't have time to let the dough rise, well, be prepared that the dough will rise in the oven.

Your pizza stones have to be preheated before you cook on them. Put the one you are going to use first into your cold oven on the lowest rack. Turn the oven to 450 degrees for about 10 minutes. Sprinkle some flour on the large, flat surface you will be rolling the dough on. Take the ball of dough and put it on the flour. If you have already kneaded the dough, then here is where you shape it. (Look at the dough ball and decide how big a pizza you are making. One dough ball, about the size of a softball, is one family-size pizza. Pull it in half to get two mediums.)

It's tough to get a perfect circle with just a rolling pin. Do the best you can. When you roll the dough out, don't try to make it too thin. It's too difficult to handle, even with the paddle. When you have the shape and thickness you want, then sprinkle corn meal on the pizza paddle and slide it under the pizza dough.

Now start loading up the pizza. This is it. The basic formula is tomato sauce first, then grated cheese, then whatever else you want. Sausage, pepperoni, hamburger, bacon, pineapple, nasty little fishes, olives, any other type of cheese, tomatoes, peppers, spinach—be creative—be prepared to share. When you're done loading up, then slide your masterpiece directly onto the hot stone. (If you are going to make more, then put another pizza stone into the oven and let IT be warming.)

Cook for about 25 minutes at 450 degrees. Start checking at about 15 minutes (it all depends on the thickness of the dough and how much you loaded it). When the dough starts to brown to your satisfaction, that is the moment it is probably done. Use the paddle and slide it under the pizza. Transfer the cooked pizza to a large plate or cookie sheet or cutting board. It'll be hot.

If there are multiple pizzas in queue, then everyone will want to sample yours. That's most of the fun really. And it is so much more delicious than you can imagine. This is better than stone soup. Much, much better.

FUNERAL PIE

FOR HE ON HONEY-DEW HATH FED

INGREDIENTS (MAKES 1 PIE)
- 2 deep-dish pie shells (make 'em if you can—buy 'em if you can't)
- ½ c chopped walnuts (But any self-respecting Texan knows it's better to use pecans. Break them up by hand. Take a little care in this.)
- 2 c raisins
- 1 c orange juice
- 1 c water
- ¾ c and 1 Tbsp sugar
- 2 Tbsp cornstarch
- 1 tsp allspice
- 1 Tbsp lemon juice
- 1 egg

PREPARATION

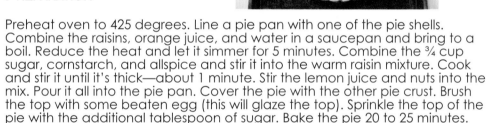

Preheat oven to 425 degrees. Line a pie pan with one of the pie shells. Combine the raisins, orange juice, and water in a saucepan and bring to a boil. Reduce the heat and let it simmer for 5 minutes. Combine the ¾ cup sugar, cornstarch, and allspice and stir it into the warm raisin mixture. Cook and stir it until it's thick—about 1 minute. Stir the lemon juice and nuts into the mix. Pour it all into the pie pan. Cover the pie with the other pie crust. Brush the top with some beaten egg (this will glaze the top). Sprinkle the top of the pie with the additional tablespoon of sugar. Bake the pie 20 to 25 minutes.

Here's the deal: the recipe I copied says serve it with whipped cream or ice cream—but no after-funeral meal I've ever been to had whipped cream or ice cream. No, you use the little clear plastic fork you were just using on the potato salad and you eat this pie as-is, by itself. If the crust was not homemade, then it is permissible to leave those pastry edges unchewed.

Belief

Sleeping with the light off is one of the things
I should be better at. I should be better
by now at a lot of things. Filing papers.
Cooking rice. Forming opinions about God.
Not being able to articulate why
red-headed women mean so little to me.
I should be better at so much of this. Life
is linear, like a string, or a long piece
of wood, and everything we do is just a
scratch on it. So does it matter that I don't
know the name of the little white flowers in
my yard? That's a question. I seem to have more
questions. Is this what getting old is? I should
be better at this. I should be better at
loving someone. I should be better walking
through the dark. Last night someone I trust took me
by the hand and led me outside. Along the
telescope of her arm she showed me Venus
shining bright, hanging like a promise. And she
told me some of the other stars. She knew lots
of them. This is one of the things I should be
better at by now I said. I should trust. You
will get better she said. I should be better
at loving you I said. You have a faith deeper than
mine. She looked at me and smiled and said Venus
will be back tomorrow. Now, let's go cook some
rice. I will show you your faith, my faith. I will
show you, in the dark, what you are still good at.

ALL THAT WINE IS

All that wine is I give to you.
The sweetness, the tart,
the immediate awareness on the tongue.
Do not spend time thinking about
this gift I give you, this metaphor.
Do not think about what else wine brings.
I do not bring you those things.
And besides, I don't know very much about wine.
Not really. I can't tell a merlot from a pinot
and am ignorant about regions and verticals.
In addition,   I cannot afford a wine
that would   be worthy of you.
So perhaps I will not   give you everything that is wine.

Maybe I should   give you the stars.
Yes. The stars. I know a little   more about the stars.
I have more experience there.   I was looking at the stars
long before I tried wine. And   it cost me nothing.
So I will give you everything there   is about stars.
Except their names. Do not ask   me their names.
Or where the constellations are.
I am sorry I brought up stars.

It would also probably be best for you to be aware
that I will not be bringing you anything
related to multi-syllabled-named-flowers,
Horses, European chocolates,
cuts of meat from a butcher I have never visited before,
or anything that has another language as part of its title.

I can only bring you my words.
And my hands. These hands. I know these hands.
I have always had them. I can vouch for them.
And maybe also I will bring you a hamburger
from a really good place I know.
These are three things that I know are true.

So, let's sit outside, tonight, and eat our hamburgers.
I will read you this poem. Then I will hold your hand.
There will be a million stars out there.
It will not be important I do not know their names.

NOTES

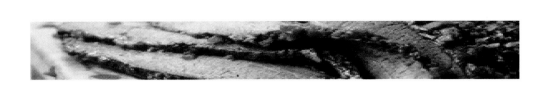

2006 Texas Poet Laureate

RED
STEAGALL

FORT WORTH

POET'S BIO

A native Texan, Red Steagall graduated from West Texas A&M University and is best known for his forty-five years in the entertainment business—writing over two hundred songs, touring and recording twenty-two albums, and having his own radio show, but he has published poetry only in the last twenty years. He currently ranches in Parker County, Texas, where in addition to his entertainment schedule, he is involved in numerous equine related activities.

In 1993, Texas Christian University Press published Red's first book *Ride for the Brand*. In 2004, *Cowboy Corner Conversations*, a collection of interviews from his *Cowboy Corner* radio show was published by State House Press, McMurry University. These interviews are what Red's poetry is all about.

Red's music is going strong. Released in 2006, *Here We Go Again* features duets with Reba McEntire, Toby Keith, Larry Gatlin, Charlie Daniels, Neal McCoy, Charley Pride, and Ray Benson. He is currently the host of *In the Bunkhouse with Red Steagall*, seen weekly on RFD-TV.

Each year since 1991, Red has hosted *The Red Steagall Cowboy Gathering*. This authentic western event, which draws thousands each year, features a ranch rodeo, chuck wagon cookoff, youth poetry contest, youth fiddle contest, youth chuck wagon cook-off, western swing dances, cowboy music and poetry, a trappings show, and horsemanship clinics.

You might even find some of his recipes there.

BEDROLL

There's a hole in the wagonsheet big as my head
Where coosie run under a tree.
Last week it rained and poured right in that hole
Probably nobody noticed but me.

'Cause that was the mornin' I jingled the horses
It rained and my bed was just fine.
But it was the first one to go in the wagon
And the rest of em stacked up on mine.

Last winter we put a new floor in that wagon
We planked it with tongue and groove oak.
She's tight as a drum and won't leak a drop
So the bed on the bottom got soaked.

Now canvas is good about turnin' the dew
As long as it's stretched the right way.
But I guess something happens, it sorta breaks down
Sittin' in water all day.

Your bed's usually warm and a nice place to be
A cowpuncher's private domain.
But it's colderin' hell in a bedroll that's wet
You're better off out in the rain.

So I put on my slicker and sat by the fire
Burned all the dry wood in the stack.
The fire made me drowsy—once I dozed off
And woke up in the mud, on my back.

Just before sunup I crawled in that bed
Couldn't sleep 'cause my feet were so numb.
Then coosie was cussin' I burned all his wood
So I got up and gathered him some.

Now I ain't one to argue and create a fuss
And I don't get my head in a fog.
But it's taken a week for me to get her dried out
And last night I slept like a log.

COOSIE'S DIP

INGREDIENTS

      6 avocadoes, prepared and seasoned for guacamole
          (or purchase prepared in refrigerator section of grocery)
      1 large can (30 oz) refried beans
      ¾ c picante sauce, divided
      1 c sour cream
      1 c mayonnaise
      1 package taco seasoning mix
      ¼ can chopped black olives
      1 4-oz can green chilies
      1 bunch green onions with tops, sliced
      1 tomato, diced
      2 c grated cheddar cheese
      chopped lettuce (optional)
      cilantro for garnish

PREPARATION

In a 9x13 glass dish or similar, spread a thin layer of finely chopped lettuce.
Then spread the following layers in this order:

      beans (creamed with ¼ c picante sauce)
      guacamole (thinned with ½ c picante)
      mixture of sour cream, mayo and taco seasoning
      onions
      tomato
      chiles
      cheese
      olives

Garnish w/cilantro sprigs and serve with tortilla chips or Fritos Scoops.

SOURDOUGH, BEEFSTEAK & BEANS

The top of my tarp sure is heavy this mornin'.
These Pendleton blankets feel nice.
It's a good thing I stuck all my clothes in my bedroll,
The canvas is covered with ice.

I just stuck my hand out from under the covers.
The mornin' air sure has a bite.
It was warm as September when I went to bed,
Musta blowed up a norther last night.

The coosie's been rattlin' them ovens since four.
The horse wrangler's ready to ride.
I hear Buster and Bubba thrashin' around,
And I could git up if I tried.

But it's nice to just lay here in my warm canvas world.
And know that I'm one lucky man.
To be able to do what I like to do most,
A genuine workin' cowhand.

Yesterday I was ridin' old Toby.
I'se relaxed with my hands on my knees.
But I grabbed for the horn when a big golden eagle,
Flew out of a cottonwood tree.

It shore was a sight when he took to the wing.
Caused me and old Toby to stop.
And watched as the wind took him out 'cross the canyon,
Where he lit in a cedar on top.

Right after sunup, we jumped an old maverick.
I throwed at his horns and it stuck.
When Toby sat down and he hit the end of my line,
It felt like we'd roped us a truck.

He turned 'round and faced us, a' pawing the ground.
I thought, boy this is my lucky day.
Then he run up my rope like he's goin' to water,
We's dodgin' him every which way.

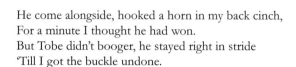

He come alongside, hooked a horn in my back cinch,
For a minute I thought he had won.
But Tobe didn't booger, he stayed right in stride
'Till I got the buckle undone.

I's tied hard and fast but I finally shook loose,
Snubbed him and left him all night.
I'll lead him in when we drive through the canyon.
This evenin' he's shore full of fight.

I'll have the wagon boss catch me old Peppy this mornin',
And I know when I tighten my kack,
I better grab a deep seat 'cause he'll buck like a colt,
Takes a good hand to stay on his back.

I don't understand why a cold frosty mornin'
Makes a gentle horse break plumb in two.
Nothin' feels worse than to land on your face
With your buddies all laughin' at you.

I had a choice, could'a gone off to college,
So you probably think I'm a fool.
But out here I'm happy, I feel more alive,
And they don't teach you to cowboy in school.

Out here a man's word means he'll do what he says
And they don't make excuses for youth.
Ain't a bed in the bunkhouse for punchers who steal
Or someone who can't tell the truth.

You know why I do this? It's my way of life.
I'm at home in my wildrag and jeans.
And I ain't got no stomach for fancy French food.
Make mine sourdough, beefsteak and beans.

Well, the wrangler just come in from jinglin' the horses.
Him and coosie are havin' a cup.
The smell of the coffee comes right through the canvas,
Guess I'd better get dressed and git up.

Chuck Wagon
Sourdough Cornbread

Ingredients

- 1 egg
- 1 c milk
- 1 c sourdough starter
- 1 c cream style corn or fresh corn scraped from the cob
- ¼ c butter, melted
- ¼ c finely chopped onion
- 1 finely chopped fresh or pickled jalapeno peppers
- ½ c shredded cheddar cheese
- 1 c yellow cornmeal
- 1 c flour
- 1 Tbsp baking powder
- 1 tsp salt

Preparation

Beat egg and milk together, add starter, corn, and melted butter. Stir gently, then add onion, jalapenos, cheese and all dry ingredients. Stir until just blended. Pour into well-greased cast iron skillet. Cook covered over hot coals or bake uncovered in 400 degree oven for 35-40 minutes until golden.

THE CODE OF THE WEST HASN'T CHANGED

The horsetrap is empty, the saddle shed's gone.
The gate barely hangs on the post.
The road to the big house is covered with weeds,
A dead cottonwood moans like a ghost.

The people who ranched here and called this place home
And pasturing on some other ground.
Maybe they've gone on to greater rewards
Or drouthed out and moved into town.

Whatever the reason there's nobody here.
And it looks like it's been a long while
Since anyone cared if this place was alive
But I can look back with a smile,

'Cause I can remember the twenty-odd years
That I rode for this outfit with pride.
Shore 'nuff good people, they treated us fair
And gave us good horses to ride.

And there was young Rusty—we called him the kid
Tho' he wasn't much younger than me.
He was killed in the cow work at Willow Springs Camp
When a bronc ran him under a tree.

And the triangle roan, when he was a colt,
He would try ya' each time you got on,
But once he quit buckin' and I got him lined out,
Was the best friend that I've ever known.

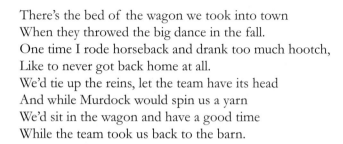

There's the bed of the wagon we took into town
When they throwed the big dance in the fall.
One time I rode horseback and drank too much hootch,
Like to never got back home at all.
We'd tie up the reins, let the team have its head
And while Murdock would spin us a yarn
We'd sit in the wagon and have a good time
While the team took us back to the barn.

They've fenced the big pasture and divied it up
Into places that won't run a cow.
It shore breaks my heart to remember it then
And see what they've done to it now.

The big thicket's gone off the cedar-top flat
Where the wagon would stay for a week.
I shore miss old camp cookie's sourdough bread
At the roundup on Cottonwood Creek.

I wonder what happened to Curley and Bill,
Cotton and Cody and Slim?
And Murdock, the wagon boss, where has he gone?
I shore took a likin' to him.

I reckon they're workin on some other range
And their horses may not buck as bad.
I bet they're still cowboyin', at least in their minds,
And relivin' the fun that we had.

I'm sure that the years have reshuffled my cards,
And the hand that I play's rearranged.
But I'll die believin' we had a good time
And the code of the West hasn't changed.

Oven Barbecued Brisket

Ingredients

NOTE! MEAT MUST MARINATE OVERNIGHT BEFORE COOKING

4-5 lb brisket
1 tsp onion salt
1 tsp celery salt
1 tsp garlic salt
½ of 3½-oz bottle liquid smoke
salt and pepper to taste
3 Tbsp Worcestershire sauce

Editor's Note: Shown is a 9 lb brisket. Double spices and Worcestershire. Increase smoke to 2 oz.

Preparation

Trim most of fat from brisket; place in pan deep enough so that foil placed on top of pan will not touch meat. Sprinkle meat with onion, celery and garlic salts; pour liquid smoke over brisket. Cover with foil; marinate in refrigerator overnight.

Remove foil and sprinkle with salt, pepper and Worcestershire sauce. Cover tightly with heavy duty foil and bake 4½ hours at 275 degrees. Mix sauce ingredients in small pan and simmer 10 minutes. Cool brisket slightly and then thinly slice across the grain, with electric knife preferably. Pour sauce over sliced meat and return to 350* oven for 30 minutes. Freezes well.

Homemade BBQ Sauce

Ingredients

> ½ c ketchup
> ¼ c water
> ¼ c brown sugar
> 1 Tbsp vinegar
> 1 Tbsp liquid smoke
> 1 Tbsp Worcestershire sauce
> 1 Tbsp chili powder
> ½ tsp black pepper
> ½ tsp small onion, chopped

Editor's note: The brisket was ready after 6 hours at 285 degrees. We sliced it immediately and spooned the sauce on top. Extremely tender. A double batch of sauce was made and the onion was substitued with the same amount of onion flakes.

NOTES

STEPHEN FROMHOLZ

JUNE 8, 1945 - JANUARY 19, 2014

EL DORADO

POET'S BIO

Steven Fromholz attended North Texas State University. Thereafter a stint in the U.S. Navy sent him to the West Coast, where he began to write poetry and music, play clubs, and subsequently launch his music career after finishing his day's work for Uncle Sam. He settled in Austin, becoming a Texas legend not only for his songwriting, poetry, and performing, but as a community activist. In the 80s, Fromholz began entertaining on rafting trips in the Big Bend area of Texas, later becoming a river guide and white-water expert. He was inducted into the Texas Music Hall of Fame in March, 2003. He returned to writing music and poetry and entertaining publicly after a massive stroke. His doctors had declared him "a walking miracle!" Exactly four years to the very day after the stroke, Fromholz stood in the State Capitol of Texas Chambers and was named Poet Laureate of his beloved State of Texas.

Fromholz has two daughters, Darcie and Felicity, and is grandfather to Felicity's son Zoe. He lived in West Texas, where he ranched with his companion Susan, and said he'd finally found his peaceful, beautiful, contented niche in the world.

Victim of a hunting accident in January of 2014, he was a consummate poet/singer/songwriter/entertainer and the ultimate Texas gentleman, a proven example of hardcore Texas grit and beloved by fans from babies to great, great grandparents. Texas will miss him.

THE LAST LIVING OUTLAW

You just might encounter his mangy old carcass
And he might look a million and he might look like hell,
In a beer joint in Beaumont or at Neiman Marcus,
His lawyer allows how he cleans up quite well.

He lives by his wits and his wiles and his ways,
He lives with his memories etched on his face,
He may live forever
And he may live for days.

He's the last livin' outlaw, he's the last rolling smoker,
Sees life kind of southpaw, he's a nocturnal joker.
His best friends are barmaids, he's a pawnbroker's pal.
Let's drink to the last livin' outlaw!

He knows all the back roads from here to Kentucky
From haulin' those lovely colitas and bales.
He was contraband careful, uncommonly lucky
'Til a judge replaced smuggling with two years in jail.

He's wise to the ways of turnpikes and diners,
From spending his days
In a red/white Freightliner,
From Tulsa to Memphis to North Carolina.

He's the last livin' outlaw; he's a sixties survivor
He's an old diesel driver, still got a quick draw,
He still loves the highway—it left him alive!
Let's roll with the last livin' outlaw!

He's a honky tonk hero and always a gentleman.
He's just a rake and the ladies are leaves.
He's been married once . . . has a daughter named Gwendolyn.
She sends him letters he rarely receives.

He's a hit with the ladies, he can dance on a horse.
He doesn't fear fightin' but avoids it of course.
Well, he once loved his wife—
Probably loved mine and yours!

He's the last living outlaw, he's a Friday night dancer,
He'll soon be a grandpaw; he's a lifetime romancer.
The ladies all love him for the light in his eyes-
Let's drink to the last living outlaw!

CHIMAYO COCKTAIL

"RAISING ONE FOR THE LAST OUTLAW"

INGREDIENTS

    1/2 c unfiltered apple cider

    1 oz good gold tequila

    1/2 oz cassis (black currant liquor)

    1 tsp lime juice

PREPARATION

Shake well, serve on ice with an apple wedge if desired.

And there ya have it!

Editor's Note: These are really good. Must use unfiltered apple cider or juice.

FONTANA CHEESE QUICHE

INGREDIENTS

    1 Favorite Pie crust

    1/2 lb. Fontina Cheese, cubed

    4-6 oz. roasted and peeled New Mexico Green Chilies, diced

        (canned chilies will suffice)

    3 green onions, chopped finely

    4 large eggs lightly beaten

    1 c heavy cream *(mas o menos)*

    1/2 t salt

    1/4 t fresh ground pepper

PREPARATION

Preheat oven to 450 degrees. Prepare pie crust and bake in preheated oven
for 5 minutes. Spread onions, cheese, and chilies in a slightly baked pie crust.
Combine eqgs, cream, and salt and pepper. Pour over chilie-cheese mixture.
Bake for 15 minutes at 450 degrees. Reduce oven temp to 350 degrees and
bake for 10 minutes or until quiche is firm in the center. *Buen Provecho!*

Blackened Ginger Bread

1	cup rich black coffee (HOT)	Blend
1	cup Blackstrap Molasses	
1	cup Brown Sugar	+ cool slightly
1	cup butter (Room Temp)	Mix with
2	squares unsweetened Chocolate	
4	Eggs (Beaten)	Blend
1	Tspn Mexican Vanilla	

2½	cups flour	Sift
1	Tspn Salt	all these
1	" Cinnamon	Dry ingredients
1	" Ginger	Together.
1	" Nutmeg	
1½	Tspns Baking Soda	

Stir Dry into Wet & beat 'till smooth.

Pour into buttered pan or pans + bake

@ 325° for 1 hour or until done.

Enjoy. Frost lightly, if you must.

S Tremholz

71

DEAR DARCIE

Intro: G   D   C
       G   D   G D/F#
Dear Darcy, here's a letter from a guitar,
Em   A   C
He told me I should sing his song for you
                  Am
And I should say it is from him;
               C
He'd like to tell you where he's been.
 G   D   C
But Daddy says it better when he sings.

     G   D G D/F#
Dear Darcy, how's your mama? Are you happy?
                    Em   A   C
Can a guitar make a living where you are?
                     Am
Well, your Daddy's band and me,
                C
We're just playing to be free.
 G   D   C
But I still miss you listening to my strings. (Stop)

Chorus:

D   C   G
Dear Darcy, can you see the wind blow by?
C   D   C   G
Covered up with snow like lookin' in a diamond's eye.
C   D   C   G C
Dear Darcy, can you see the Northern lights?
D   C   G
Dear Darcy, it is really mostly night?
D
Are you all right?

Chorus:

```
G                      D      G D/F#
```
There's a letter on the table from a guitar.
```
   Em              A          C
```
To a little girl who's gone four thousand miles,
```
                         Am
```
And when she opens it she'll see
```
                    C
```
There's a postscript just from me
```
G D C (STOP)
```
With all the love a letter's line can bring.

```
   G
```
It'll say Dear Darcy
```
D                          G
```
Do you miss me like I miss you?
```
                 Em    A        C
```
Are you old enough to know the way I feel?
```
Am                                      C
```
Am I man enough to see, how much in you there is of me?
```
G                      D        C
```
And do you still believe your Daddy's real?

Darcie helping her Dad get ready for a photo shoot. —*Photo by George Brainard*

Now, here's another little poem I'd like to share with you. . .

Roscoe, the flatulent rat

Had no need to fear the old cat.

For when Roscoe farted

The feline departed

And that was the end of that.

When Roscoe ate Stilton Frommage

His farting came in a barrage.

He stayed in the house

With a little brown mouse

While the old cat slunk off to the garage.

The little brown mouse was a she mouse

And Roscoe thought he'd be her he mouse.

But she knew he was a rat

And that he hung his hat

Whereever he found a free mouse.

So Roscoe was back where he started

But not in the least broken-hearted.

He still had his hat

And the silly old cat

That Roscoe thought must be retarded.

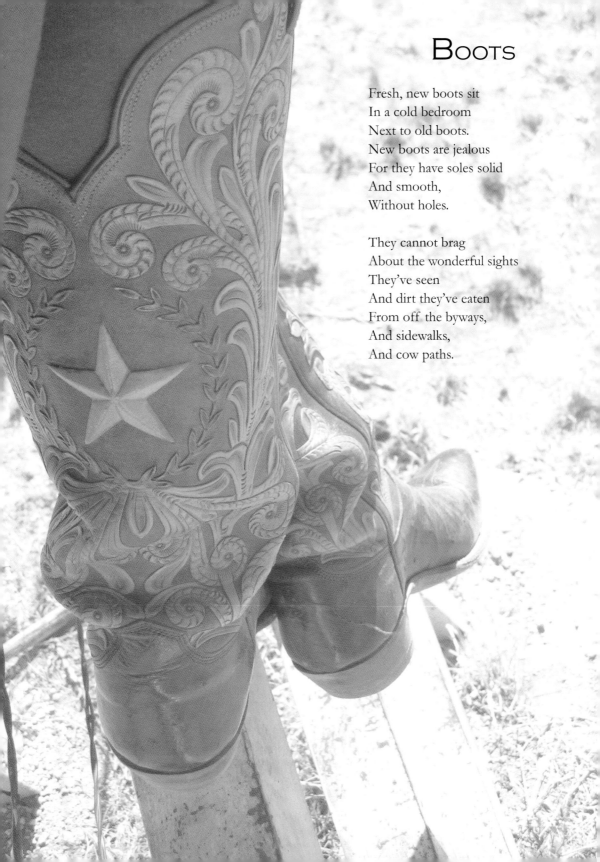

BOOTS

Fresh, new boots sit
In a cold bedroom
Next to old boots.
New boots are jealous
For they have soles solid
And smooth,
Without holes.

They cannot brag
About the wonderful sights
They've seen
And dirt they've eaten
From off the byways,
And sidewalks,
And cow paths.

NOTES

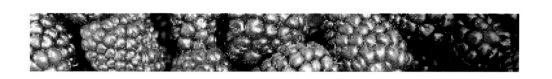

LARRY
THOMAS

HOUSTON

Poet's Bio

Larry D. Thomas, the 2008 Texas Poet Laureate and a member of the Texas Institute of Letters, has published several critically acclaimed collections of poems, most recently *Uncle Ernest* (Virtual Artists Collective, Chicago, 2013). Among the numerous awards and honors which he has received for his poetry are two Texas Review Press Poetry Prizes (2001 and 2004); the 2003 Western Heritage Award (Western Heritage Museum, Oklahoma); the 2004 Violet Crown Book Award (Writers' League of Texas); and selection as the 2002 Houston Area Barnes & Noble Booksellers Author of the Month. His *New and Selected Poems* (TCU Press, 2008) was a semi-finalist for the National Book Award. Thomas currently resides in Alpine, Texas, with his wife, Lisa.

Rattlesnake Roundup

At sunrise, bands of gunless hunters

stud the bleak West Texas landscape,

clutching forked sticks, wide-eyed at openings

of cap rock dens, shoving vees

    behind the venom-bulged heads of vipers,

    bagging their catch in coarse tow sacks

    for the trip to the town coliseum,

    to pits teeming with fugues of fierce rattling

        where handlers press fangs against lips of jars,

        milking poison, and butchers section cuts

        for deep fryers, cooking sweet, snow-white meat

        for the leathery mouths of old townsfolk.

DEWBERRIES

They grew in brambles
along a barbed-wire fence.
Within days that summer
and right before our eyes,
like our own strange bodies
ripening with pubescence,
they'd turn from greenish-white

to pink, pink to red,
and red to dark purple.
The night after we picked them,
our tongues still blue with guilt,
the maps of our skin
covered with hundreds
of thin red highways

scribbled by their thorns,
and stinging, we'd picture,
before we fell asleep,
the buckets brimming with them
on Grandma's kitchen table,
pregnant with the promises

of muffins and a cobbler.

DEWBERRY MUFFINS

INGREDIENTS

      1 c fresh dewberries, cut in half (may substitute blackberries)

      1 ¾ c all-purpose flour, sifted

      ¾ tsp salt

      ¼ c white sugar

      2 tsp baking powder

      2 eggs

      3 Tbsp melted butter

      ¾ c milk

PREPARATION

Preheat oven to 400 degrees. Sift flour, salt, sugar, and baking powder into a medium size bowl. In a separate bowl, beat the eggs. Add the melted butter and milk to the beaten eggs. Combine the wet ingredients with the dry ingredients and mix until moist. Gently fold in dewberries. Fill each well-greased cup of muffin pan until two-thirds full. Bake 20 to 25 minutes.

Fried Pies

To make the filling, the mothers

cut the ripened apricots from their stones,

slice them into strips, soak them in pots of water,

cook them, add sugar and cinnamon, and cook them

again till they reach just the right consistency.

As the filling cools, they roll out the dough

for the crust, cut it into round pieces

they spoon the filling into the middle of,

fold them neatly in half, seal the curved

edges, pressing them with the tines of a fork,

and deep-fry them in bubbling lard

to a perfect medium brown.

As the pies cool on the table,

the children close their eyes and salivate,

picturing a thousand ripe apricots

dangling from the branches of the trees,

each a fuzzy, rosy, yellow sun

setting in the maw of the night.

Apricot Fried Pies

INGREDIENTS
- 1 lb fresh apricots, peel and cut into pieces (may substitute preserves when not in season)
- ¾ c white sugar
- 1 c water
- 1 tsp vanilla
- 1 tsp cinnamon
- pie dough

PREPARATION

Place the apricot pieces, sugar, and water in a saucepan. Cook on low heat until apricots are tender and the mixture has thickened to preserve consistency. Set aside to cool and add vanilla and cinnamon.

Pie Dough

INGREDIENTS
- 2 c flour
- 1 tsp salt
- $2/_3$ c shortening
- 3 Tbsp cold butter
- 4 Tbsp water

PREPARATION

Combine flour and salt. Mix one-half of shortening and butter into flour mixture using hands until it is the consistency of small pellets. Add the other half of flour mixture and mix until it is crumbly. Sprinkle water over the dough and lightly blend. Add an additional 1 teaspoon of water and form the mixture into a ball. On a floured surface, roll out the dough to approximately $1/_8$ inch thickness. Lay a salad plate flat on the dough and cut a circle around it. Place some of the apricot mixture on one side of the dough, fold dough, and crimp with a fork to seal it. Fry the pies in hot oil until they are golden brown. Remove pies from the oil and drain on a paper towel. Let pies cool since they will be very hot. You may want to dust the outside of each pie with a little sugar and cinnamon while still hot, but it is not necessary.

CRABBER

Ninety years of Galveston sun
reign in her flesh like a bronze tattoo
needled indelibly into her face,
arms, and legs. Her throat's adorned
with a choker of perfect sharks' teeth,
hard, imperturbable as her squinty gaze.
Daily, during the summer months,

she takes fresh chicken necks, yanks string
around them tight as tourniquets,
grabs net and bucket and prances
the few yards from her shanty to the surf.
With nothing but her sense of touch, she works
her stringed necks like a master, easing
the net under the bellies of greedy crabs

and shaking them violently
to the bottom of her bucket. As she waits
for the next strike, she fixes her gaze
on the sea, matching its brute indifference
with the iciness of her stare,
the crabs clacking in the bucket like dominoes
shuffled by the age-blotched hands of old men,

fueling her dream of dropping big blue males
into a bubbling stockpot flaring her nostrils
with crab-boil, reddening their blue
in but minutes, their sweet, white meat
but briefly satisfying to her appetite
as the seven feckless husbands
whose cremated bodies she's dumped into the sea.

DROVERS

by the trail boss,
just dollar-
a-day drovers
content to subsist
on biscuits,
bacon,
beans and,
if lucky, a slurp
or two of syrup,
the cattle
they wrangled
too valuable
at the railhead
for racks of ribs
or brisket
on the trail,
just dollar-
a-day drovers
driving herds
from Texas
up to Kansas
for months, up
to where a month's
pay fizzled
to bottles
of rotgut
and slipshod
quarter-hours
with a whore.

OVER BARBECUE

Too old to work cattle, they gather
once in a while around a campfire

fueled with dead mesquite to swap tales
over barbecue. One asks the eldest

how many steers he supposes
he's eaten in his life. He muses

a few seconds and answers surely
a sizable herd. Their dentures

clack tearing meat from spareribs, loose
as the clothes on their gaunt, bent frames.

Each chomps on, adding another head
to the ghostly, sizable herd

roaming the horizons of his marrow,
lowing in the pasture of his soul.

The Buffalo's Famous
BBQ Baby-Back Pork Ribs

EQUIPMENT PREFERRED
> Weber "Genesis" gas grill (or any other gas grill)
> Use mesquite chips for grill smoke box
> (soak chips in water for 30 minutes before placement in box)

INGREDIENTS
> 1 thawed rack of baby-back pork ribs
> 1 bottle of McCormick Grill Mates Pork Rub
> 1 bottle of Sweet Baby Ray's Barbecue Sauce

PREPARATION

Apply rub liberally all over the surface of the meat (including the underside). Pre-heat grill to 250 degrees. Place rack in middle of grill (with convex/meat side of rack on top). Close grill lid. Do not open lid while cooking. Cook indirectly (no flame directly beneath the rack) for one hour.

Apply barbecue sauce liberally/thickly over entire rib rack. Place rack in middle of grill with convex/meat side of rack on top. Close grill lid. Do not open lid while cooking. Cook indirectly (no flame directly beneath the rack) for an additional hour.

Place cooked rack in pan and cover with aluminum foil, letting the meat "rest" for twenty minutes. Slice rack into individual ribs. Chow down!

Reminders: The total cooking time is two hours (the first hour without the sauce) Do not open the grill lid while the rack is cooking. Maintain the cooking temperature at 250 degrees.

NOTES

PAUL RUFFIN

WILLIS

Paul and Jack on Hog Vigil in Willis.

POET'S BIO

Paul Ruffin, Texas State University System Regents' Professor and Distinguished Professor of English at Sam Houston State University, is Editor of *The Texas Review* and Director of Texas Review Press, both of which he founded. He holds a PhD from the Center for Writers, University of Southern Mississippi.

Ruffin is the author of two novels, five collections of short stories, four books of essays, and seven collections of poetry, and the editor or co-editor of fifteen other books, including works on Steinbeck and Texas novelist William Goyen. His fiction, poetry, and essays have appeared in such journals as *Alaska Quarterly Review*, *Boulevard*, *Georgia Review*, *Hopkins Review*, *Michigan Quarterly Review*, *New England Review*, *Paris Review*, *Poetry*, and *Southern Review*, and his fiction and poetry have been featured in a number of college texts, including Norton's *Introduction to Literature* and *Introduction to Poetry*, and Harcourt-Brace's *College Creative Writing Handbook*. In addition, his work has been featured on NPR.

Currently Ruffin lives in Willis with his wife, Amber, and their dog, Jack. He continues to write vigorously, with three books expected out in 2014. He writes a weekly newspaper column, *Ruffin-It*, which has appeared in newspapers in Texas, Mississippi, and Alabama.

Unlike pampered Marines Parsons and Rattan, who rode in helicopters and landing craft, Ruffin spent his Basic and Advanced Infantry training with the U.S. Army. He had to walk.

How to Get the Most Mileage From Your Chicken

One of the positive aspects of growing up poor in rural Mississippi is that you learn how to utilize as fully as possible the elements of diet that are available to you, from vegetables to animals hunted down or raised for slaughter. These lessons typically stick with you long after you no longer have to worry about which chicken to choose from the pen.

Let us consider, for example, how much mileage one can get out of a chicken if managed properly.

Amber and I will buy one of Kroger's free-range five- to six-pound girls, wash her thoroughly, remove the little package from the body cavity (retaining the neck for further use), and then brine her. Brining is an essential step if you want to end up with a chicken that is tender, tasty, and juicy. If for some perverse reason you don't, then forget about brining her and get on with the roasting.

Now, brining is marvelously simple, involving nothing more than putting a gallon or so of water in a large pot, dumping in a cup of coarse salt and a quarter cup of sugar, stirring until everything is dissolved, and then submerging the bird for six to eight hours. Rinse and dry her off when the brining process is finished and let her sit overnight in the refrigerator, covered only with a piece of paper towel. Though I understand the process by which brining works its miracle, it is a bit too complicated to try to explain here—the point is that it works.

After her overnight chill, lay the bird on a platter or tray and melt two or three tablespoons of butter, then brush her all over, top and bottom and ends and sides, with the butter, followed by a liberal application of Accent, Lawry's Seasoned Salt, onion powder, garlic powder, and black pepper. (Throw on anything else you want her to wear on the oven date.)

Lay the old girl on a piece of aluminum foil large enough to wrap her totally when you're ready to slide her into the oven and get together your ingredients for injection. That's right, Bubba: you're going to do this right and inject Bertha with what I tell you. Otherwise I'm wasting a whole lot of strokes here. Frankly, a well-brined chicken will be moist enough, but it's not just moisture that we're after here—it's flavor too.

I use a heavy-duty stainless-steel injector that easily breaks down for cleaning in the dishwasher and will hold around three ounces per charge.

The first step in preparing a good injection mixture is to melt three tablespoons of butter in six ounces of apple juice. Stir in a teaspoon of Better Than Bouillon chicken base, a dash of onion powder, and a dash of garlic powder. Blend it all really well in the microwave.

Inject the mixture in several areas of the breast, thigh, and drumstick, using as few injection points as possible and moving the needle about beneath the skin so that she won't look like you've shotgunned her—you don't want the injection liquid squirting out a dozen holes.

Once you've finished your injection, replace any of the surface prep that's been rinsed off, cradle the chicken in two layers of foil, and lay her in a large Dutch oven on a rack with at least three quarters of an inch of water in the bottom. Then add a pint or so of chicken stock made from Better Than Bouillon directly to the bottom of the foil the chicken is resting in.

Slide the bird uncovered into a 220-degree oven, insert a temperature probe with remote, and let her cook slowly until she reaches 180 degrees, basting the chicken every couple of hours. When the alarm goes off, remove the temperature probe, turn the oven on Broil, and add a little extra browning.

After you have Bertha browned nicely, take her out of the foil she's been roasting in and remove some of the drippings to make gravy to serve with rice and some of that fine breast and thigh meat. If you don't know how to make chicken gravy, it's not my fault you ain't from the South.

Go ahead and eat most of the breast meat, because what you're about to make requires less of it than anything else on the bird. Make a little chicken salad if you've got enough left over.

OK, let's say that you get two good meals out of the main meat of the chicken, so she's already paid for herself, but if you discard what's left of her without going on through with my plan for Bertha's remains, you might as well just give up on wringing all the juices out of life.

See, all that nice brown skin and all the little pieces of meat still clinging to the bones are the best part of the taste left in her. Truss me (joke there). You are going to need some supplemental chicken meat, so be certain to have on hand four large thighs with skin and bones. You'll understand this better by and by. (As we used to sing in church.)

Put into a boiler three quarts of chicken stock made from Better Than Bullion, slide in the remains of Bertha: I mean everything *left* of the bird, including the neck that you saved from that cute little package the chicken folks hid in her for you. Yeah, she'll look like roadkill, but it's taste we're after here, not a beauty crown. Bring her to a good hard boil and render her down for a couple of hours, then let'r simmer a bit and cook off some of the liquid.

Now, take those four large chicken thighs, put them in a couple of quarts of chicken broth made from Better Than Bouillon and boil them for hour or so, and then let'm simmer a bit.

Once it's clear that you've boiled all the taste out of the carcass that you're likely to coax out, pour the whole mess through a fine strainer and set the juice aside. Go ahead and turn the heat off on the thighs and let them sit there in their savory juices.

The most tedious part of this process is separating the edible meat from the not-unless-you're-at-the-road-kill-hungry-stage meat. It's a really important step, though, unless you want to hear your mate griping about the little bones later on.

Once you have the meat separated, dump it into a large stock pot with the juice left over from the carcass rendering, and pour in the remaining juices from the foil you cooked ol' Bertha in.

Now strain the thighs, add the juice to the main pot, then discard the bones and fat from the thighs and throw the good meat into the pot. The reason you use thighs with bone and skin is that you extract a whole lot of fine chicken juice, and the dark meat gives the dish a whole lot more flavor than more white meat will. There are those who will argue about this, and they're not lying—they just don't know any better.

Whoopeee, now you have that fine pot of chicken juice and meat ready to be fired up for the next ingredient: the dumplings.

Purists among y'all out there will argue that you don't really have genuine chicken and dumplings unless you go through the long and painful process of making your own dumplings. Once upon a time, it was the thing to do. Today you go to the store and buy packages of Mary B's Open Kettle Frozen Dumplings, which are already in little floured strips that must be cut or snapped to size and introduced to that marvelous meaty broth you have going in the pot. These things can be a little messy to fool with, but they are worth the effort, and they taste just as good as yo' grandmomma's dumplings.

Take the whole 24-ounce package, cut or break the dumplings to size, and chunk'm in to cook at a low boil for a little less than an hour, and you are set for some fine eating. (If, by the way, you want to thicken them, add a little corn starch; if you want to thin them, add a little water.)

Folks, you'll get another two or three days out of Bertha if you follow my instructions here, and you'll love every molecule of her. Truss me. (Yeah, again.)

SMOKING A BOSTON BUTT
WITH BAKED BEANS

OK, flip through any recipe book on cooking outdoors these days, and you're going to find instructions on how to fix the best pulled pork this side of Paradise, and almost every one of them will yield a palatable dish: It's hard to fix pulled pork without a fair measure of success. I cannot claim that this recipe is vastly superior to all others, but it's the best I've come up with, and I've tried plenty.

As you might imagine, the first step is choosing the meat, and it's also the easiest. Catch Boston Butts on sale, six- to eight-pound range, bone-in, and buy one. While you're at it, buy a large can of Bush's Country-Style Baked Beans. If you don't have a good marinade and/or don't know how to prepare one, put that in the basket too. I use Claude's BBQ Brisket Marinade, which I order by the six-pack from Amazon. You'll need a small bottle or can of apple juice, too, and some honey mustard dressing. If you don't already have onion and garlic powder, Lawry's Seasoned Salt, and a few jars of Better Than Bouillon (chicken and beef) at home, you don't need to be cooking meat anyhow, but go on and buy some if you are ready to get serious about this dish.

I can assume that if you are intending to smoke a butt, you have a smoker, but I don't have the right to assume that you have a meat injector and remote thermometer at the house, though you should. This recipe requires both.

OK, now to get down to the serious issue of preparing the butt for smoking. Make certain that you have a metal grate to put the meat on, because you are going to lay it directly on the grate so that it can take full advantage of the smoke boiling up from beneath. You also want a large bowl of water at the bottom of the smoker to provide adequate moisture with the smoke. You can smoke meat in almost any kind of cooker, but those with a vertical smoke chamber and side-mounted firebox seem to me to be the most serviceable for most homeowners' needs.

Remove that big old chunk of pork roast from its package, rinse and dry it off, and then put it in a two-gallon Ziplock bag and dump in a bottle of Claude's Marinade. Roll it around a bit, then lay it in the refrigerator and periodically turn it to redistribute the marinade.

Alrighty, now. Cometh the morning, sun or not, take the BB out of the refrigerator and drain off all that marinade, pat the meat dry, then lay it on a tray for the final prep. This, folks, is an important step.

Melt three tablespoons of butter in a measuring cup, add four ounces or so of apple juice and two ounces of Better Than Bouillon stock, sprinkle in some onion and garlic powder, warm everything up in the microwave, mix well, and then inject the butt on both sides, using maybe two full charges of this magic liquid. Again, the meat will turn out just fine without injection, but you'll appreciate the added flavor dimension.

Next, wipe the butt dry and lay it on a clean tray and liberally smear it all over (and I do mean all over) with a good brand of honey-mustard dressing. This helps add a little extra taste to the bark, but more importantly, it provides a coating that your dry-rub will stick to. In a big bowl, mix your dry-rub, and this can be a grand combination of ingredients of your choosing (recipes all over the Internet) or a good commercial concoction like John Henry's Texas Brisket Rub. Now pat this mix on heavily and press it into the honey mustard coating. You're going to have a Boston Butt in a cocoon of rich spices just waiting for the smoker.

Get your smoker up to 220 degrees—I prefer hickory to maintain that temperature—and leave the butt on the top rack, uncovered and lying directly on the rack, using the middle rack for your beans. (WARNING: DO NOT DO ANYTHING ELSE BEFORE YOU FINISH READING THROUGH THIS WHOLE THING.)

Be certain that you have at least half a pan of water in the bottom of the smoke chamber. Spritz the BB with apple juice/chicken stock every hour or so and let it smoke at that steady temperature of 220 for a minimum of five hours, during which that roast is going to absorb all the smoke taste it needs.

After the requisite smoke exposure, take the butt out, seal it in aluminum foil (after inserting remote thermometer), put it in a Dutch oven with half an inch of water in the bottom, and slide it into a 190-degree range oven, and let it lie there in its own sweet, gentle simmer for ten to twelve hours. I like to put mine in the oven when we go to bed and wake up to that marvelous aroma the next morning. If the internal temp has not reached 190 degrees after that length of time, jack the temp up a bit and give it a little while: I promise you that it will reach the magic 190-degree mark in short order. 190 is the point of perfection: no more, no less.

When it reaches 190, take it out, spread open the foil, let it sit a few minutes, yank out the bone and discard it, then let the pulling begin, mixing the meat with all those juices that have accumulated in the bottom of the foil. When you've finished with your Mississippi Bone Picker job, dump the meat into a container for refrigerating. Eat what you can for a few days and freeze the rest.

Now, baked beans are a requisite side dish for pulled pork. Potato salad is a given, but anybody with half a dozen Southern blood cells can make passable potato salad. Baked beans, though, are another issue.

First of all, forget that notion that you have to start from scratch to make baked beans. No, no, no. Let other folks do the scratching, and you take advantage of the basic recipe they've come up with and improve on it. I let Momma Bush and her family do all that initial work of picking and shelling and washing the beans and mixing in the fundamental spices and doing the canning for me. My time is worth a lot more than just over a buck a can.

After you have your Boston Butt situated in the smoker and start bringing things up to temp out there, take one of their 28 ounce cans of Country Style Baked Beans and dump them into a large cast-iron skillet and heat them up. Sauté a medium-size onion, finely chopped, in a quarter-cup of Better Than Bullion Chicken stock and add them to the beans, along with two heaping tablespoons of brown sugar. Stir everything in well.

Now then, take about four extra-thick slices of Nueske's applewood-smoked bacon (they sell these in twelve-ounce packages on their web site) and dice them on a cutting board, making little quarter-inch cubes of unforgettable flavor, and brown them in a skillet and add them, along with a tablespoon of the bacon grease, to the beans. Stir all this in too.

See, you already have a vastly-improved version of Bush's baked beans, almost good enough to fight the family over, but Honey Chile, the best is on the way.

Grab you an oven mitt and snatch that cast-iron skillet of beans up and lug them out to the smoker and set them on the rack below that Boston Butt, which is just beginning to feel the heat. The beans are now above the water bowl in the smoker and directly below the BB, so you can imagine what's about to happen.

As the BB begins to heat up and ooze its goodness at every pore, those juices drip right down into that skillet of beans beneath. I don't have to tell you what that adds to the taste of them.

After three or four hours of sitting in that 220-degree smoker, enjoying a constant drip-drip-drip of goodness from that Boston Butt, with an occasional stir to mix things up, those beans are ready for the table, but you can leave them out there for five or six hours, and it won't hurt a thing.

Don't look for these beans to be syrupy so that you have to slurp what's left in the bowl. They are thick and rich and . . . aw, just make'm and check'm out y'self.

Now, I can't fault you for going to the trouble of making your own baked beans from scratch. You may have the time and inclination to devote to a dish that I can just about guarantee you won't rise to the level of taste of this one. You don't want a Throw-Down over this recipe, I promise.

A SUMMER MEAL WORTH CONSIDERING

You know how it is when the Dawg Days of deep summer have set in and it's hot as the hinges of hell, the birds don't want to fly, and the dull-eyed squirrels are bushy-tailed in the literal sense only? Even though you're starving, you don't want to fire up the grill or heat up the kitchen, so you try to decide what might be nice for lunch.

The idea for this light summer meal came from my days in the waters of the Gulf off Mississippi. I married into a fairly large fishing boat and got to do lots of fishing (and some shrimp trawling) with my father-in-law. For over thirty years, my wife and I spent several weeks a year over there with the inlaws. (I divorced out of the boat a few years ago.)

What I am proposing here is a modified Mississippi Gulf lunch, designed to be quick and tasty and filling and *healthy* and requiring little more in the way of cleaning up than stashing some bottles and sardine cans and paper plates. And you don't have to worry about a fish making a reel scream just as you're getting ready to take a bite.

The focal point of this surf-and-turf dish is a can of sardines, preferably two-layer brislings packed in olive oil. (These days I buy them by the case from Amazon.) They have a peel-tab top, easily opened, and the little flat can is fine to leave them lying in until you scoop them out to eat.

You must also have crackers (Club or saltines), some strips of Extra-Sharp Cheddar, strips of onion (red or white or yellow), and a container of mayonnaise (which needs, of course, to be kept in the fish box or refrigerator after opening). Beer is the final ingredient, any kind you like.

You gotta be outside, and it needs to be hot enough that the beer becomes as important as the sardines. One reason you have to be outside is that your wife—and kids, if you still have any hanging around—are going to gripe about the smell of sardines. I know that there are

98

women and kids out there somewhere in the vast dimensions of this country who like both the taste and smell of sardines, but the only place I've observed this phenomenon was in European countries bordering the North Atlantic or Mediterranean. Likewise, I've never met a cat who wouldn't be willing to fight you to death over your sardines, and this is where the onions really come in: you can lay on a table or bench in the back yard an open can of sardines with a mine field of slices of onion around it, and no cat will go near it.

OK: you're outside and it's hot, and you have your ingredients together. Now cometh the glorious process of building your tasty little treats and scarfing them.

Take a cracker and smear it with a bit of mayonnaise mortar, lay on a strip of cheese, and press it into the mayonnaise. Now extract from its olive oil bath a sardine and arrange it on top of the cheese, no matter which direction it's pointing, since it'll go down nicely in either direction.

Finally, take a slice of the onion and drape it over the whole shebang, look around you to make certain no one is watching, and then shove it into your mouth and let your molars do the rest. Chase each one with a minimum of two slugs of beer.

This recipe will take care of your hunger and cool you off, and your taste buds will be quarreling over which ingredient tastes the best. Finally, it is not likely that you'll end up having to share this meal with anyone in the immediate household.

Now Let Us Speak of Cornbread . . .

Amber is a heck of a dessert cook, but she leaves most of the savory dishes to me. Over the years, I've gotten pretty good with a few recipes: spaghetti, fried catfish, lasagna, roast, pulled pork, steaks, etc.

Now, cornbread is cornbread is cornbread, some might say, but that's just a garden-variety lie: some cornbread is better'n other cornbread, a fact that I would argue to my last breath.

My recipe was lifted somewhere along the line years ago and improved on. That's how most new recipes come about.

Now, here are the ingredients the cornbread calls for:

> a cup of cornmeal
> two eggs, lightly beaten
> half a cup of vegetable oil
> eight ounces of sour cream
> ten ounces of frozen (or canned) cream-style corn
> a tablespoon of sugar
> three teaspoons of baking powder
> half a teaspoon of salt
> half a teaspoon of black pepper

You mix all these ingredients together and put them in a greased black skillet and bake for 35 minutes on 350 degrees.

When it comes out, you'll be mightily impressed. If you want to be mightilier (couldn't resist) impressed, listen up.

That cornbread is to live for, no matter what, but you can fool with the recipe a bit and make it a lot better. First of all, I don't know about you folks out there, but I have never dumped cornbread out of a cast-iron skillet a time in my life that a little scab of crust didn't pull loose and make the cornbread look ugly, like it had been in a fight and lost. It's downright irritating. Grease it any way you like, whether the skillet is seasoned properly or not, and the cornbread will come out marred. Doesn't hurt the taste of it one whit, but after all that trouble, you are entitled to a picture-perfect round of cornbread.

Here's a tip, something I learned from the Husk Restaurant in Columbia, South Carolina. You take a tablespoon of good bacon grease and put it in a cast-iron skillet you've heated for about five minutes in a 400 degree oven. It'll sizzle and slide around and make all kinds of fuss. Just make sure that you coat every square millimeter of that skillet up to the edge.

Put it back in the oven for another minute or so and get it and the bacon grease so hot that the batter shrieks when you dump it in, which is what you'll do the very second you take out the cornbread and taste it. Even out the batter in the skillet and put it back in the oven for about thirty minutes on 350.

But, hey, that's just to make the crust taste mighty fine. You're still likely to get a few little tags of crust pulling loose. Here's where my second tip comes in.

No matter how much I love cast-iron cookware, sometimes you gotta get practical and snatch up a non-stick Calphalon skillet, send it through the bacon-grease treatment, and let it do its thing. The cornbread will never complain, I assure you, and neither will your wife or anybody else who sees it lying there, a perfectly browned cornbread round, unmarred by scabs and tags.

As long as we're talking bacon grease, let me suggest that instead of the half cup of vegetable oil, you heat up a quarter cup of some really fine BG, like Nueske's, which I prefer to Benton's because it isn't nearly as salty, and mix it with a quarter cup of vegetable oil. This'll give you a faint taste of bacon in the cornbread itself and not just in the crust.

Another tip: If you like a little heat in your cornbread, as we do, sprinkle some red-pepper flakes in the batter and stir it in well. A good handful of grated cheddar cheese adds another flavor dimension that doesn't detract from the taste of the cornbread itself.

Y'all can thank me later for this recipe. Good eating!

NOTES

2010 Texas Poet Laureate

KARLA K. MORTON

DENTON

Poet's Bio

Karla K. Morton is a Councilor of the Texas Institute of Letters, a graduate of Texas A&M University, and member of the Greater Denton Arts Council. Described as "one of the most adventurous voices in American poetry," she has been featured on radio, television, and in countless newspapers, blogs, and magazines. Morton's nomination has been accepted into permanent file for the National Cowgirl Hall of Fame, and she is widely published in literary journals. She has authored nine books of poetry and has established a touring ekphrastic exhibit stemming from her ninth collection, *No End of Vision: Texas As Seen by Two Laureates* (Ink Brush Press), which is a collaborative book with 2005 Texas Poet Laureate Alan Birkelbach—Morton's photos inspiring Birkelbach's poetry. Morton's work has been used by many students in their UIL Contemporary Poetry contests and was recently featured with seven other prominent authors in *8 Voices: Contemporary Poetry of the American Southwest*.

A native Texan, Morton has trekked thousands of miles across Texas and beyond—bringing poetry and the arts into schools, colleges, universities, civic groups, cancer support groups, and festivals in communities all across the States. Her forthcoming book *Constant State of Leaping* will be published by Texas Review Press in the fall of 2014.

Photo credit to Nicki Cathro with Cavern Media

Damn Dishes

Give me
lime and butter and salt and chicken
and I will make you a happy man.

Just try walking into a house
with a bird in the oven
and not fall in love

Yes, your stomach says,
this could be your life—
this woman could feed you;
could make magic from produce
and frozen chicken thighs

Later, after sex,
you walk out to bones and dirty dishes
and soft annoyance,
thinking *who's gonna clean up this mess?*

This, sir, is why
you will always be
a single man.

Mama Charlotte's Black-Eyed Peas

—from Mama Charlotte Morton King

INGREDIENTS

 1 16-oz package of dried black-eyed peas
 2 lbs Jimmy Dean sausage (I like one mild, one spicy—your choice)
 1 medium onion
 2 14-oz cans whole tomatoes—*not drained*
 3 c water
 2½ Tbsp finely chopped celery
 4 Tbsp sugar
 2½ Tbsp chili powder
 2 tsp garlic salt
 ¼ tsp pepper

PREPARATION

Soak peas overnight, keeping water at least 2 inches over the top of the peas. Brown sausage and onions together. Drain and rinse off grease in a colander in hot water. Drain water from peas. Pour all ingredients in a big pot and bring to a boil. Cover and simmer 1 to 2 hours or until tender. Best served with a big spoonful of chow-chow (see next recipe).

PARIS AS I SEE IT

—for Elise Pierce

She said what she loves about Paris
are the possibilities;
the way sunrise smells
like warm croissants,

and midnight smells like pizza.
How morning stirs the colors in the Seine,
and people prefer formal grammar,
yet french in full view on the Metro;

how apartments are ranked
Housman and postwar;
how dogs are everywhere
but children rarely seen;

how current events take second
to pure butter, roasted chicken
and chocolate crepes;
how champagne comes before the wine;

and the locals smile as she butchers
the language, because that's exactly
how they like it—rich and tough,
but perfect with a nice bottle of red.

Chow-Chow

*—from my grandmother, Laura Mae Moseley,
via Lone Star Gas Company during WWII*

Ingredients

1 qt green tomatoes (about 5 medium-sized tomatoes)
2 sweet green peppers
2 sweet red peppers
2 large mild onions
1 small head of cabbage
¼-½ c salt
3 c apple cider vinegar
2½ c brown sugar (packed)
1 tsp dry mustard
1 tsp turmeric
2 Tbsp celery seed

Preparation

Prepare vegetables and chop or grind. Add salt and let stand overnight. Drain and press out all liquid possible. Rinse with clear water and press out all liquid again. Add other ingredients and bring to a boil over full flame. Reduce to simmer and cook for 2 hours. Stir mixture frequently. Pour into hot, sterilized, clear canning jars and seal. Makes 10 to 12 pints.

PICKING UP THE ACCENT

My husband calls me a chameleon,
says that everywhere I go,
I pick up the accent,
sounding just like a local
within a few months of living there.
I had no idea I did that.

I wonder if it's the food...

But maybe that's what
finding your own voice s all about.
Maybe it's not so much
about where we're from,
but where we've *been*
that matters.

We ingest every experience.

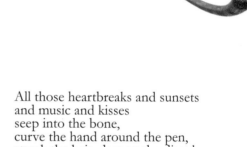

All those heartbreaks and sunsets
and music and kisses
seep into the bone,
curve the hand around the pen,
streak the hair, deepen the dimples,
and lilt the vocabulary
like quick whiskey to the tongue...
We can't help but bring it *all* to the table.

It took me 2 hours and 42 years to write this
poem.

Perhaps one day, I'll travel to the moon
and learn the accent of silence
from the barren craters and powdered Tang,
and mix it all in
with the Florida sunshine and citrus;
the Carolina society and sugar;
the New Orleans *'Laissez les bon temps rouler'*
and gumbo;
the cowboy boots and Tex-Mex;
(and all those other places I've yet to know)
and *then* see what voice emerges
the next time I come to the table
and sit down to write a poem.

CHERRY COKE JELL-O SALAD

—from my mother-in-law, Adell Gambrell Morton

INGREDIENTS

- 1 large package cherry Jell-O
- 1 can tart pitted cherries
- 1 c sugar
- 2 c water
- 6 oz Coca-Cola
- 1 small can crushed pineapples (drained)
- ¾-1 c chopped pecans

PREPARATION

Boil cherries, sugar, and water for one minute. Pour over Jell-O powder. Set in refrigerator. When slightly thickened, add other ingredients, put in 9x13 inch pan, and return to fridge until ready to eat.

JELL-O HEALING

Four days without food
leads to a feast of Jell-O—
bright red strawberry happiness.

I like how it forms to the cup,
the way my spoon curves out its own shape.
I feel it slide the long driveway into the stomach—
the cool opening of the belly.

I do not know how God merges everything in our life;
every little detail of our magnificent body;
but some wee stomach guard ushered it right in
to be divvied up and delivered in little straw baskets—
to the muscles, the blood, the heart.

My daughter said her vegetarian friends
don't eat Jell-O—
said they're made from horse hooves . . .
and I smile at the thought of all those cleft cuticles
ground up and stomping through my body;

the rage of Earth and Grass and Sun;
glorious snorting, steaming steeds;
those four perfect legs;
that broken-out gallop;
that unsaddled strength.

Brownies

—from my mother-in-law, Sara Morton

Ingredients

¾ c butter
3 squares unsweetened chocolate
3 eggs
1½ c sugar
1 tsp vanilla
¾ c flour
½ c pecans (optional)

Preparation

Heat oven to 350 degrees. Use a small square glass pan (unless doubling, then use long glass rectangular pan). Melt together butter and chocolate. Beat in eggs and sugar. Add in other ingredients. Bake at 350 for 30 to 40 minutes, then check with toothpick. I like the toothpick to come out clean when inserted at the edges of the pan and to come out gooey when inserted in the middle! Best brownies ever. A great recipe to double.

MUSIC BOX LUNCH

This is why we travel this way—
with a blanket and ice chest,
and a map rolled in King Ranch

leather—for these endless acres
just beyond the Brazos, joyfully
trespassing in the round shade

of hay bales, sharing cold chicken and plums
and brownies . . . . Let the traffic have its
fast food, rushing to destinations,

ours has always been about the road—
the line; the curve; hands clasped
between the seats—our love,

devouring time like twigs in a fire . . . .
There is a rhythm here—a lid, lifted
off a box of magic—music wound

by the circling black wings above us;
hay bales placed like perfectly scored
pins; the comb of the wind, plucking

each golden ball—a song of time
that's meant to be opened;
a song of the moment—

when it's all about the dappling sun,
the smell of the river, and
a thousand miles of road yet to come.

NOTES

2011 Texas Poet Laureate

STATE ARTIST AWARD

DAVID PARSONS

CONROE

Poet's Bio

David M. Parsons is the recipient of many honors and awards, including a National Endowment of Humanities Dante Fellowship to the State University of New York, the French-American Legation Poetry Prize, and the 2006 Baskerville Publisher's Prize from TCU for an outstanding poem published in their literary journal, *Descant*. He holds six writing awards from the Lone Star College System, and he was named Montgomery County Poet Laureate for 2005–2010 and Finalist for Texas State Poet Laureate for 2010. Parsons was elected to The Texas Institute of Letters in 2009.

A former Marine, Parsons attended The University of Texas-Austin and Texas State University, where he holds a BBA. After several years spent working in business and advertising and coaching baseball and basketball at Bellaire High School, he received an MA in Creative Writing and Literature from the University of Houston, where he studied with such poetry luminaries as Edward Hirsch, Robert Pinsky, Richard Howard, Stanley Plumly, and the late Howard Moss, long-time poetry editor of *The New Yorker*.

He is founder and co-director of the Montgomery County Literary Arts Council's Writers In Performance series and chairman of the Conroe Arts Alliance. After serving for seventeen years on the Conroe Commission on the Arts and Culture and over fourteen years as Chairman, the city honored him, proclaiming October 7, 2010, Dave Parsons Day in Conroe. Parsons has four grown children and lives with wife Nancy, an award winning artist and graphic designer.

116

REBA

My late mom, Reba Lanette Kierbow Parsons, was by far the best cook in our entire extended family. When she reached her eighties, we urged her to put together her recipes in a book. The project was undertaken by my wife Nancy, and the result is a family treasure. The booklet includes not only her recipes but also a little family culinary history. She grew up on a farm in Georgia, and the book begins with a description of her family's existence at that time. The following is a portion:

"Everything that was used in these and all recipes of the Kierbow family were grown and made on our big farm in Carroll County (Georgia). They grew all the corn, wheat, etc. for meal and flours; grew their own spices; made their own yeast; and of course, churned the milk for butter and cream. There was no refrigeration, so we lowered all the perishables into a well with rope and pulley. We had no cabinets in our big kitchen, so we used wooden safes with screened doors for bread, pies, cakes, etc. Weekends, the neighbors would come and the adults would sit and talk about their crops and us kids played on the huge front porch, which was piled with cotton that all of us had to pick during that particular season. However, in the winter we had other parties, mainly hog killing parties. The neighbors would gather at our house and kill hogs and dress them, so we had all of the ham, sausage, etc. that we needed for the entire winter. The women would can sausage patties and stuff the hog guts with sausage; that was my favorite—link sausage. All the meat was hung in our smoke house and it stayed there all winter. The men would kill the beef cows and handle the storage the same way. Today when I hear of food poisoning, I often wonder how we stayed so healthy."

Most of the recipes in Mom's book are used by our individual families; however, the following was NOT one of them . . . but I loved this and thought it worthy of having and re-membering.

CORNBREAD & CORNBREAD DRESSING

A Southern favorite, sometimes made with black-eyed peas for traditional New Year's Day for luck. The first of Mom's recipes that everyone was interested in having was her cornbread dressing. Though Nancy, being from St. Louis (we are a culinary mixed marriage), liked the cornbread dressing, and we now enjoy both the Yankee dressing as well at Thanksgiving.

INGREDIENTS FOR CORNBREAD

> 1½ c buttermilk
> 1½ c corn meal
> ½ c flour
> 2 eggs
> 1 tsp salt
> ½ tsp baking soda
> ½ c bacon grease

PREPARATION

Mix all together and pour into greased pan. Bake at 425 until brown. Let cornbread set overnight.

INGREDIENTS FOR DRESSING

> ½ stalk celery
> 1 chopped onion
> 2 tsp poultry seasoning
> 2 tsp sage
> salt and pepper to taste
> 1 egg
> chicken broth – enough to moisten the cornbread
> cornbread crumbs – enough to fill the bird

PREPARATION

Mix all of the above until soupy and pour into baking dish. Bake at 400 until brown.

GRITS AND HAM

My first memory of any food remains one of my favorites. My mother put a plate-sized serving of firmly concocted grits in front of me and then made a smiley face with a knife in it. She filled in mouth and eyes with red-eye gravy and cut up ham slices for the "hair" of the face. I don't make the smiley face any longer; however, I often have grits and fried ham . . . adding a little coffee to the ham grease to generate the red-eye gravy.

Ingredients

    1 c grits

    2 c water

    salt and pepper to taste

    a slice of ham

    ham grease

    enough strong, black coffee to make red-eye gravy

Preparation

Boil grits and water until done. Add salt and pepper. Fry ham slice until slightly browned and thoroughly heated. Cut ham julienne style into hair strips either before or after cooking. Pour enough coffee into the remaining ham grease to form a gravy while stirring continually to remove any cooked-on pieces of meat. Fill individual bowls with grits and cut a smiley face on each. Arrange ham "hair" over eyes and fill the mouth and eye depressions with gravy.

The Greek Ancient Recipe

Asparagus was first cultivated about 2,500 years ago in Greece. In Greek culture, Asparagus represented the spear of love and was held in high regard by Ancient Greeks as an aphrodisiac. Here is the original recipe that I patterned mine after. The Liquamen, also called garum, was a fish sauce prepared by leaving fish parts out in the sun for several months with sufficient salt to prevent rot. The result is a clear fish sauce that was used to spice both Greek and Roman recipes. If Liquamen or a commercial substitute is not available, Nuoc Nam or other oriental fish sauces can be used.

Ingredients

   1 dish of asparagus (usually less than a market bundle)
   wine to make mashed asparagus pass through a sieve and to add
       to the sauce
   Liquamen or other fish sauce
   pepper, lovage, fresh coriander, savory
   onion
   oil
   6 eggs or more
   a generous handful of shredded sharp cheddar cheese

Preparation

Put the asparagus in the mortar and pound. Add wine and pass it through the sieve. Pound pepper, lovage, fresh coriander, savory, onion, wine, liquamen, and oil. Put purée and spices into a greased patina and break eggs over it when it is on the fire so that the mixture sets. Sprinkle finely ground pepper over it and serve.

DAVE'S QUICK ANCIENT MEAL

I also have a favorite egg dish that I discovered from ancient recipes offered on the Frugal Gourmet. I have a personal favorite rendition of the formula as follows:

INGREDIENTS

> 1 bundle of asparagus
>
> 1 tsp olive oil
>
> 1 clove garlic
>
> 6 eggs or more
>
> a generous handful of shredded sharp cheddar cheese

PREPARATION

Break asparagus spears into bite-size pieces and sauté in olive oil with garlic. When they turn bright green, pour off excess olive oil and fold in at least six eggs, beaten. Scramble with the asparagus until firm and set aside. Sprinkle your favorite cheese (mine is sharp cheddar) over the top and cover for about 3 minutes. Delicious for any meal.

Note: A side of bacon, ham, or sausage tops it off for me.

EASY CAJUN SALMON WITH ASPARAGUS (OR BROCCOLI)

My favorite quick healthy meal: Brush wild caught salmon steaks with extra virgin olive oil (both sides). Sprinkle generous amount of Tony Chachere's Original Creole Seasoning on steaks. Bake at 450 until flakey. Braise asparagus in olive oil and garlic until crisp (not limp).

Two Dogs Howling at the Moon

for Rusty Wier 1944 -2009

I will always remember the last time I saw you,
at your *angel's,* Tricia's crowded Plano townhouse

and how, after our four hours of harmoniously
catching-up on thirty some odd years of lost time,

I read you my poem *The Pride*, about that pack
we ran with—we thought we were lions, we were

more wolves or stray dogs—reliving those old stories
of growing up together wild in the enigmatic sixties

in South Austin, like our Tequila drinking contest
when I came home from the Marines, how I passed

out hearing you strumming to *Rave On*, learning
later, you had quickly followed me to the darkness

falling dead-drunk onto your beat up old guitar,
like some faithful warrior falling on his sword.

As our visiting ebbed, you played for me the second
of your three new songs, saying, *"I'm still writing—*

*can't stop doing that one thing—we're like those two
old dogs in my song, David, we writers just keep barking*

and howling at that ole' moon," your voice still
inimitably valved despite the chemo and the thousands

of songs poured out like manna to the many hungering
audiences of the nightlife you so loved and I remember

at that moment thinking how Li Po is said to have so
adored that great luminous orb that he perished, when

after a night of heavy drinking, he fell into the lake
attempting to embrace the dazzling antediluvian body, tumbling

head-long and alone into the deep ink of oblivion,
or perhaps, the masked reflections of an eternal light

and how you, after sailing through countless gigs
and seas of Agave, one complimentary shot at a time,

were now arduously floundering to make the best of each
of these last painfully clumsy egregious moments,

like you always have, with that distinctive dancing
twinkle in the weathered squint of those smiling blue

eyes, eyes still fully alive in my memory, still dancing—

I suppose every human passion holds within its core
the germ of something lethal to its being and yet,

somehow, interwoven with the potential of rapture.
Tonight the sheer linen curtains of my bedroom seem

to be tossed by the blurring energy of the moonlight
bouncing glowing stones across the dark water of our pool

as the ceiling fan circles in its perpetual waving orbits
and I can hear my daughter's tiny lap dog underneath

my small dinghy of a bed gnawing like memories
on a T-bone scrap from dinner, he is at that phase

where all the meat is flayed away and one can only
hear the sound of bone against bone as he is working

into a rhythm in his ceaseless mastication, creating
his own unique kind of wild, raw and satisfying music.

I Would Give You The Single Strawberry

Not because it is the end of May: the season—
or that in the 17th Century William Butler said,

It is doubtless God could have made a better berry,
but doubtless God never did; or that the delicate

uniquely heart-shaped berry has been heralded
through the ages as a symbol of purity, passion

and healing; or because of Shakespeare's adornment
of Desdemona's hankie; or that Madame Tallien

of Napoleon's court would crush 22 pounds in a fine
basin and bathe in the glory of the luscious ruby juices;

nor because of its shape and color, it was the symbol
for Venus: Goddess of Love; or that it was widely held

by Romans to alleviate symptoms of melancholy, fainting,
kidney stones, halitosis, attacks of gout, liver and spleen;

not even the legend that if you are lucky enough
to have a double berry and share it with one

of the opposite sex, surely true love will follow;
not even that they are the only fruit carrying their seeds

boldly on the outside like the regality of knights of olde.
I would give you the single strawberry as a kind of communion
offered in recognition, remembrance and celebration of our brotherly and
sisterly spirits;

moreover, as a reminder: strawberries are not harvested with machines, their small
bodies

being so very delicate, human hands must carefully harvest each berry; and as we
savor it, let us meditate together on the visions

of the multitude of pickers—people like you and me—bending under brutal sun in
the rote of work, taking each unique berry

with measured grace, with reverent aplomb—I would give you a single strawberry
because, despite all that has perished

and been lost the past year, we
have lived to see . . . to taste another glorious spring!

FRIED GREEN TOMATOES

For my late Aunt Jeanette Kierbow

I cannot recall one conversation I had
with her, just the cool dignified kindnesses
when I visited from Texas her tiny neat
modest Bremen, Georgia, home with photos
of Liberace placed like one might display
important family members or iconic leaders

maybe saints; the sumptuous fried green tomatoes
she introduced to me one day after coming home
for lunch from a morning of sewing on the assembly
line at her life-long Sewell Suit Factory job, yet, her
neatly modest and homely presence, after over five
decades of not having seen her, returns at unexpected

times, her jet black hair and awkwardly attractive
tall rangy angular body with those remarkable eyes—
those icy agates set in that smooth pale oval face,
eyes that seemed to look directly through you
as brown eyes, with all their warm charm
seem never to do . . . like the difference between

the kindred eyes of dogs and the inescapable
and ineffable combination of chill and thrill
that is stirred subtly deep within our own animal
depths, when unexpectedly one might glance up,
finding our gaze has becoming locked in—frozen
in the rapt mystical hunter eyes of a cat—

now an enduring memory of that first titillating tug
of the visceral, formative instincts of the fine keening
of the pure quintessence of discovery: new, green—fruit.

NOTES

2012 Texas Poet Laureate

STATE ARTIST

AWARD

JAN
SEALE

RIO GRANDE VALLEY

Poet's Bio

Jan Seale, a native Texan, was the 2012 Texas Poet Laureate. She lives in McAllen in the Lower Rio Grande Valley of Texas. She attended Baylor and holds degrees from the University of Louisville and North Texas State University.

Seale's poetry has appeared in such journals as *New America, The Cape Rock, Descant, Nimrod,* and *Kalliope,* as well as in many anthologies and on the NPR program "Theme and Variations." Her poems are collected in nine volumes.

Her prose writing has appeared in such places as *Texas Monthly, The Yale Review,* and *The Chicago Tribune.* Seven of her short stories were selected for PEN/Syndicated Fiction Projects, with two broadcast over National Public Radio. Dramatic works by Seale have been produced in Boston, San Angelo, Wichita Falls, Austin, Salado, Edinburg, and McAllen.

Seale held a Creative Writing Fellowship through the National Endowment for the Arts in 1982. She is a member of the Speakers' Bureau for Humanities Texas as well as a member of the Texas Institute of Letters.

As for her cooking, she estimates she has prepared approximately 173,000 plates of food in her lifetime. This includes having fed three hungry sons for 18 years each and a hungry husband for a great many more years.

Eating Texas

It's taken a long apprenticeship
to make waffles in the shape of Texas.
First there were mountains over Waco.
Then the Panhandle sank.

A few more false starts when
the Red River swamped Oklahoma
and the Rio Grande dripped into Mexico.
Now I can make perfect ones.

All I have to do is take care
to stop pouring the batter a little shy
of El Paso, Dalhart, and Texarkana.
For some reason, Brownsville needs more.

Otherwise, my grandchildren complain they
don't have the tail of Texas to bite off.

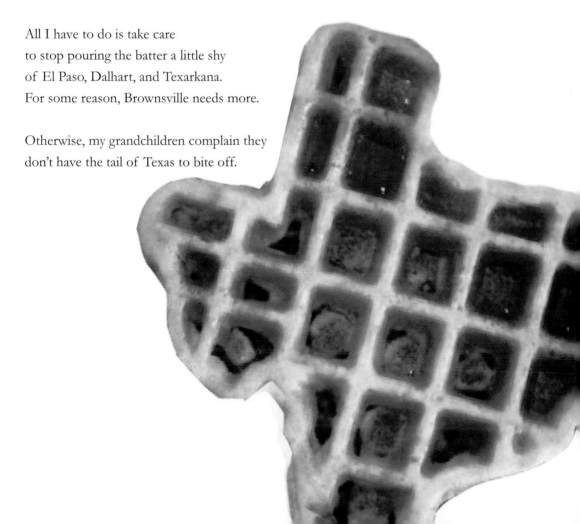

Swooning-Dinner-Guests Roast

Ingredients

- 3-4 lb chuck roast
- 4 cloves of garlic
- 1 Tbsp dried oregano
- salt and pepper to taste
- a twig of rosemary (optional)

Preparation

Heat the oven to 450 degrees. Peel the garlic and cut each clove in thirds lengthwise; poke these slivers into the meat. Rub salt, pepper, and oregano well into both sides. Place the meat in a roasting pan, lay the rosemary on top and cover tightly with foil. When the oven is as hot as the witch's oven in Hansel and Gretel's tale, put the meat in and let it cook for exactly 30 minutes. Don't forget it! Then lower the heat to 250 degrees and cook it for 3 hours. Check for tenderness and if necessary, cook it another hour. Throw the rosemary away.

If you have time, drain into a bowl the broth accumulated from cooking the roast and let it sit in the freezer about an hour until the fat congeals on top. Virtuously skim off this widow-maker and throw it away. Now you have some nice broth to combine with that in the gravy recipe.

GRAVY

2-3 Tbsp cornstarch

2 c canned beef broth

1 small can mushrooms, drained

healthy dash of red wine

Put the cornstarch in a cup and add enough cold broth to dissolve it. Combine all the broth and cornstarch and cook it until it thickens, stirring constantly. (Humming helps. Think of it as a mindfulness exercise. At this time, you might want to sample the wine to be sure it is fit for the final touch.) If the gravy doesn't thicken, use a little more cornstarch dissolved in cool water. Finally, add the mushrooms and wine (about glub, glub). Cut your tender roast into single helping sizes, place in a shallow serving dish and pour the gravy over it.

Don't count on any leftovers.

Limes, Anyone?

The other day, we looked out our front windows and saw a neighbor under one of our Mexican lime trees, shaking away. My husband went out. "Caught you!" he said, laughing. And the man, who has gleaning rights, agreed. Seems he needed a few of the spiky little fruits to prepare his tilapia for guests that night.

It's harvest time again. Our two front-yard Mexican lime trees are groaning under the weight of their fruit. Every year in July, we experience a virtual wave of neighborly love. Morning and evening walkers stop by, presumably just to chat. But their eyes travel upward. They lick their lips as they remark how large and healthy our trees are.

Yesterday we asked our yard crew to trim one branch that was threatening the roof of our carport. A little while passed and the doorbell rang. Could the worker have a sack please? The branch was loaded with new limes. He'd pick them off and give them to us—and, uh—if we didn't want them, he'd be glad to take them off our hands.

For several years we have enhanced the good will of our local friends and even our long-distance relatives by means of these little green edible golf balls. Mexican, or Key lime differs from the larger Persian lime, with its thick skin and dumbed-down flavor. Loaded with all manner of nutritious elements—polyphenols, antioxidants, fiber—Mexican limes not only give a health benefit but pack a wallop of eye-squinching sour flavor that complements scores of dishes.

My husband bought these two trees as saplings on the side of the road about ten years ago and planted them in our front yard. He continues his paternalistic attitude toward them as they dominate the entire area. During the fruiting seasons—twice a year—he goes at least once a day like Little Red Riding Hood with his basket to pick up the ripe ones that fall to the ground.

In the kitchen, his farmer's pride evaporates. I am allowed to sort, wash, squeeze, freeze, and prepare dishes with them. Sometimes we think we have exhausted uses for them, and then we find another. The obvious ones get a heavy workout at our house. At high season, friends entering the house are bold to inquire, "Got any of that limeade you make?" I have to admit, through the years I've developed a cravenly delicious formula: 1 cup fresh squeezed lime juice dissolving 3 cups sugar (not a misprint), then 3 quarts of water. If I have it, a crushed sprig of mint goes into the pitcher.

For some reason, lime juice makes almost any dish taste better. It is the ultimate flavor enhancer. We squeeze it into soups, use it in salad dressing and salsas, and garnish papaya, avocado, watermelon, and banana. Okay, it makes these a bit mushy if you don't eat them right away.

That's because lime juice is the ultimate tenderizer. Give chicken or tuna an hour under this mesmerizing liquid and the result could make you famous.

And after all the edible uses, lime juice can be used to wash vegetables, gargle, doctor mosquito bites, cure toe fungus, and rinse hair.

We here in South Texas are the willing recipients of many things we have nothing to do with procuring. Mexican limes love us because of our alkaline soil, having come across the world from Southeast Asia. These tart little orbs got handed off to the North Africans and near Easterners by Arab traders. Somewhere along the way—probably at a common proselytizing meal—Crusaders took them to Palestine and Mediterranean Europe. By 1250, they were being grown in Italy and France.

Then dear old Columbus did something right: limes are listed on the bill of lading for his second voyage in 1493 to the New World. Easily grown from the seeds of the fruit, the trees were introduced into   the subtropical United States and Central America.

We here on the border naturally call them Mexican limes, rather than favoring the name given by our domestic citrus rival, the Florida Keys. Our only concession seems to be in the name Key Lime Pie.

July and August are lime-dominant months at our house. We gather a couple of thousand limes during that period. Another 500 or so come off in the second season,

around Christmas. And what on earth do two city dwellers do with all these limes? It's not as though we could eat them like mashed potatoes.

We give away as many as friendship allows. Several of our neighbors, as already indicated, are heads-up for our sharing. Others have their own lime trees, and this fact we have to keep mutually telling each other year after year.

And then there are the squeeze evenings. At some desperate point, the fridge is full of limes, gathered at a half bushel a day, and we have to "work them up," as my farming grandmothers would say.

We are on our second juicer, the first one's notched spindle worn down by thousands of acidic sacrifices. My husband mans the knife and cutting board and I stand over the machine, making a game of how fast I can place the lime half on the rotating spindle. The juice sluices out, most of the seeds caught in the holding collar. After a while, I notice I have a full pitcher and must transfer the three cups to a larger container. Eventually, I re-strain, for hardy seeds that have slipped through, and measure the juice into one-cup portions in small jars for the freezer. I know, I know, you recommend plastic bags, but these often leak, and besides, "canning" with Ball jars makes me feel ancestral and virtuous.

What I do not like is the clean-up. One may think Mexican lime juice is so sour it couldn't possibly be sticky, but it is—syrupy, ticky-tacky, filled-with-sugar sticky.

Regardless of how careful we are, the hapless little things exact their own revenge. As we work at detonation, the juice squirts and sprays. Eventually, it drips off to the floor. We make the trip to the compost with the heavy bucket of rinds—bless their little dessicated hearts—and it's back into the house to purge the counters, mop the floor, clean our glasses, and take a shower.

As I write this, I figure I have about one more week of peace before the evening juicing ritual starts. We are already heading out with gift bags of limes to the hairdresser, minister, masseur, library clerk, and exercise partners. And a few are already gently refusing them, or taking them to give to their neighbors and friends. It's a spreading epidemic.

Soon we will hang a sack on the mailbox for Oscar, our mailman. A couple of trips north will find us traveling with loaded picnic iceboxes of limes to grace our way into the hearts of relatives.

Some lime-tree owners—and there are many in our area—do not collect their limes. The ground beneath their trees is a sea of decaying yellow. I envy their lack of concern, their profligacy. My rural ancestral past does not allow me such liberties. Whatever grows and is edible, I have to harvest. (Just now, the bananas and papayas on our backyard trees are coming ripe, without any particular care except water. We have our South Texas version of a Victory Garden. And maybe we're going to need it.)

Today the limes hang quietly in the bright sunshine of our yard, in silent nanoseconds growing larger, juicier, sweeter, more sour. They're not much prone to pests—though one year chinch bugs sneaked in to initial each fruit with a little blip. Grackles tend to borrow a few for use oiling their feathers and wasps have a penchant for making black dots on their surface. Still, the season is here and there's more than enough for us and all our wildlife.

Something besides the utility of the limes keeps beckoning us to them. Is it just greed for the abundant and luscious?

In them, nature calls out far beyond our needs. They are like the stars, or grains of sand, in their overabundance. Their excessive giving is flabbergasting. They answer our need for astonishment, for admiring what is out of control. We harvest them and know the most elemental of human activities, taking the bounty of the earth.

And they put us into a community of believers. "Oh my gosh!" say our visitors, looking up into the trees and pointing. We smile and step back into the kitchen to get a bag for them.

It's Christmas in July.

GRINGO LIMEADE

INGREDIENTS
    1 c lime juice
    3 c of sugar   (1/2 may be low-calorie sweetener)
    3-3½ qts water

PREPARATION
    Place lime juice in bottom of gallon container and slowly add sugar,
    stirring constantly. When sugar is fairly well dissolved, add water. This
    is a strong mixture, but it's just right when ice is added to the glass.
    Makes about 1 gallon limeade.

GLORIA'S MEXICAN LIMEADE
Sounds wild and crazy but surprisingly refreshing and a pretty green!

INGREDIENTS
    Top stems and leaves from one big bunch of celery
        or about 8 celery stems
    ½ c water
    ½ c lime juice
    3 c sugar
    3-3½ qt water

PREPARATION

    Place the celery in food processor. Add ½ cup water and process until
    smooth. Strain the material with a fine strainer or cheesecloth to get
    ½ cup celery juice. Throw the pulp away, or save it to use creatively
    some other way. Combine celery juice, lime juice, and sugar. Stir, stir,
    stir until sugar is dissolved, then add water.

South Texas Margaritas

For one quart of frozen margaritas:

Ingredients

   1/3 c lime juice

   1 c sugar

   ¾ c water

   ¾ c Tequila

   1/3 c Triple Sec (may be non-alcoholic)

Preparation

Dissolve the sugar in the lime juice. Place all in blender and fill with ice. Zap until slushy. Make a glass for yourself and one for a friend. Go out on the porch and watch the sun go down. You will be as close on earth to nirvana as you're going to get.

Editor's note: These are great using Sonic Ice in a bag. We made the syrup mix and stirred it over the ice in the pitcher. They have been made several more times. Awesome!

I Cut Open A Papaya/
My Husband Reads His
UFO Journal

Seven months we have waited, looking into the garden
as this fruit becomes a world, at first a hard green egg,
then so slight a blush, we argue with our vision,
rely on yesterday's color, and in the final month,
wonder if it's deep gold or the sunset's bounce;
chant against the possum shinnying up the trunk,
the wasp finding entry, the grackle's stony stare.

Quince, apricot, and finally, marigold: it's time.
"I'm going to pick it," my husband says after supper,
a householder's evening chore more interesting than dishes.
He bolts out the door, twists the three-pound ellipsoid free.
I watch from the window.

Now he sits in a room nearby, reading of grays, abductees.
I split the papaya with my sharpest knife,
the sound like my water breaking with our first child.
A galaxy of black planets rushes to the light,
a hundred or two shining ova with a flurry
of green impatient sprouts. I scoop the seeds in reverence,
save them on a plate. He wants to dry and plant them,
plant them all, row upon row. Peeling,
I slice a wedge, bite the gold, lean to the sink,
the musky flesh in my mouth after all these months.
I take the other part to him.

In another dimension, by lamplight, he raises his head,
opens his mouth. He samples, blinks up at me
from inner space. Yes, he agrees, this melon planet
is unexplainable—from stick, sunlight, water, grace.

Back in the kitchen, I make conserve, stirring the pot
of saffron: papaya, pineapple, sugar, lemon.
I'm humming thanks to the woman far away
who shared this recipe; I'm barely contained
by the row of glittering jars with pretty labels.
I'm happy.

"Hmmm." I hear him sigh and shift,
likely off to the hunt, pursuing cigar-shaped airships,
enemies with slanted eyes, patterns in wheat.
Suddenly he's leaning in the doorway.
"Listen to this," and he reads from outer space.
I stand listening, sucking my sticky fingers,
our marriage hovering, listening, marking us.

Papaya Mama Cobbler

Ingredients

   4 c peeled, seeded, cubed ripe papayas
   ½ c or more sugar or artificial sweetener, to taste
         (according to sweetness of papaya) 3 Tbsp lime juice
   1 Tbsp almond extract
   1 tsp ground cinnamon
   ⅛ tsp nutmeg
   ½ box of dry yellow cake mix
   1 stick butter or margarine, melted
   ¼ cup finely ground pecans
   sprinkle of sugar
   ½ c orange, pineapple, or other juice or syrup from canned fruit

      (as needed)

Preparation

Place the cubed papaya in a large bowl and stir in lime juice, sugar, extract, cinnamon, & nutmeg. Let sit for 20-30 minutes, stirring 2-3 times. The mixture should be slushy (action of lime juice and sugar breaking down papaya). Pour this mixture into 8X13 shallow cobbler pan. If the mixture is not very juicy, add up to ½ cup of the optional syrup and stir.

Sprinkle ½ box of dry cake mix over the fruit, distributing evenly over the entire surface. Press out the lumps gently with a fork. Surface does not have to be perfectly smooth. Drizzle melted butter over the cake mix. Sprinkle on the pecans and finish with light sprinkle of sugar.

Bake at 350 degrees, uncovered in center of oven for 30-40 minutes. Keep checking until the top is light golden brown, but it may not be as firm as a regular pie or cake. Great eaten warm, cold, with or without topping of vanilla ice cream or whipped cream.

Frijoles Borrachos

(Drunk Beans)

INGREDIENTS

    1 lb dry pinto beans

    1 clove garlic (or 1 tsp minced garlic)

    1 celery stick, chopped extra fine (optional)

    1 carrot, chopped extra fine (optional)

    1 tsp cumin

    1 finely chopped onion

    1 small whole jalapeño, seeds removed (optional)

    1 ham bone (*not* raw soup bone) or 2 small pieces salt pork
        or bacon

    1 can beer, room temperature (optional)

    ½ tsp baking soda

    salt and pepper to taste

    cilantro if desired

PREPARATION

Wash beans thoroughly and place in water to cover in large cooking pot.
Bring to boil; cut off heat; allow to sit one hour. Pour off water and cover
again, this time about 3 inches above beans. Bring to boil. After 15 minutes of
medium boiling, add ½ tsp. baking soda and stir furiously. (This process and
throwing away the first water removes the "social" factor.)

Add onions, garlic, jalapeño, and ham bone. Set heat to very low, cover,
and let cook, stirring occasionally. After about one hour, add celery, carrots,
cumin. If water is low, add a cup or so of HOT water slowly. Cook another hour
or until beans are just tender. Keep heat very low, but liquid bubbling. In last
fifteen minutes, add salt, pepper, and can of beer very slowly.

Dip out the jalapeño and throw it away unless there is a craven fan of it. If de-
sired, just before serving, stir in ¼ to ½ cup chopped cilantro, including stems.
Serve in bowls; should be soupy. Hot tortillas or cornbread is good with beans.

No mas necesito!

Notes

ARE THERE PICTURES OF WILLIAM BLAKE IN AN APRON?

This connection between writing and cooking has certainly got my mind working. I have thought through all the surface connections between the two and come to the conclusion that the distribution of multiple talents is pretty capricious. It may be that Whitman could whip up a good bowl of buffalo chili or it may be Sappho cooked everything in olive oil, only the best virgin olive oil. Or maybe both of them just stumbled around and let acolytes take control of the wooden spoons. I wonder sometimes if the painter Gericault had cooking in mind at all after he painted "The Wreck of the Medusa". Did Hemingway cook all the manly fish he caught? Who knows really? We can rewrite history a little if it makes the story better, but a lot of times, basically, we just don't know if the writer was also a good cook. It just doesn't come up much. Shakespeare—good at sonnets. But at the Texas-shaped waffle machine—maybe he wasn't so good.

The point I'm making is that sometimes you can't depend on a metaphor working in all situations. A poet is like a cook. In some ways—sure. In some ways—he might stick a fork in the toaster when your back is turned—but then he will sit down and write a mean sestina.

When I give a poetry workshop I do not harbor any illusions that I am also giving a cooking class. Some things are similar, I suppose: the gathering of ingredients (pen, pad, flour, sesame seeds), studying the target market (or glancing at the picture of what the Cookie Monster cake is supposed to look like), and then, in moments of madness, writing a villanelle that breaks the rules of line count and rhymes (or, maybe instead of baking a peach pie you make a carrot pie.) That last one is pretty important: the absolute willingness to fail gloriously.

So what's the advice then, one tiny bit of wisdom that both the cook and poet can agree on? Take the risk. Nobody has to read your bad poems. Nobody has to eat your carrot pie. But you tried. A month, a year, a decade down the road when you are getting squeezed by time you might regret that you never tried to write any Irish amra. And while you're at it, try cooking some Welsh rarebit. Watch that you don't burn it.

A COMMENT, BRIEFEST OF ESSAYS, OR ANECDOTE ABOUT FOOD

Most of my friends and kinfolk love getting together to eat. A shrimp boil or fish fry on Saturday night. Cook-offs, brisket and beans and all the Habaneros you can eat. Born in the Great Depression, I thought chowing down after church was part of worship. All-day singing and dinner on the ground.

It's a wonder church people's favorite songs aren't hymns like "When the Rolls Are Served Up Yonder/We'll Be There," and "God Be With You/Till We Eat Again." A rolling stone may gather no moss, but all recipes draw wise cracks and jokes like Velcro. How lucky can Texans be? Food and music, friendships and family, the Lone Star flag and the love of God and country.

from the desk of Karla K. Morton . . .

THE RECIPE TREASURE BOX

I have moved a total of 11 times in my life—twice in childhood, once to college, then eight times after marriage. Now, recipes weren't even on my radar until I was a new wife, suddenly realizing it was up to me every night to put a dish on the table, and it was then that I received one of the greatest gifts ever—a homemade cookbook. My mother worked for months writing down those old family recipes that were always made from memory—knowing my memory wasn't so great, and worrying about the home-making skills of this newlywed!

In it are recipes like her meatloaf, chicken fried steak, peach daiquiris, great-grandma's pineapple rice pudding, my grandmother's two-pie crust recipe for one chocolate and one coconut cream pie; even simple things like how to boil an egg (on low, for at least 10 minutes, then set it aside and let it cool in the pan).

The book has grown, the old-school 3-ring binder bulging with the gems I've picked up from all my travels, and I've added two index boxes, full of treasures such as Hello Dollies—cupcakes with German chocolate icing on the inside (which took 12 years of nagging to get), or crawfish dip, an old New Orleans family recipe, which took 6 years to finally get! I guess you could call me a foodie-hound—it's no surprise when my kids come home, we all end up cooking in the kitchen—my daughter even studying to become a pastry chef.

And then there are those that I steal and tweak, like bread-pudding—morphing a combination of two great Cajun chefs—Emeril Lagasse and the classic Commander's Palace recipes. We actually got to know Emeril when his first restaurant opened in New Orleans, having the back number for the kitchen—long before his "Bam!" days! Or finally figuring out the secret ingredient (by multiple tries and failures) to Del Frisco's Steakhouse's famous tomato and onion salad. How priceless are these?

But, on every move, I never trust my cookbook to movers—I hand carry it to every new destination, much like an old storyteller, with bits of my kids artwork, and side notes and splatterings of grease and flour. It is our culture, our history; social gatherings around a table. It's where people are bound together and nourished.

I recommend getting an index card box, and a large supply of index cards to fit inside—no matter who you are, no matter what age you are. Keep them handy. If you love something, write it down—many times key ingredients get lost from time and age and extremely good wine.

Recipes are heirlooms to be passed down, generation to generation. Times will change, tastes will change, even some ingredients will change—like switching back to butter from Crisco.

Scents and smells create memories that are everlasting.

Start your own treasure box. See how rich you'll become.

146

WISDOM IN THE KITCHEN

✓ You know all the fuss about whether to use Accent (MSG) in your food or not? Forget the negatives and use the stuff: It is a flavor enhancer, lower in sodium than salt, and it makes almost every savory dish taste better. Just use it in moderation.

✓ Everyone would love to be able to find the time to make beef and chicken stock from scratch, but it's a genuine pain, so do the next best thing: take advantage of the Better Than Bouillon bases made by Superior Touch. Their chicken and beef bases are absolutely splendid. They also have fish, ham, clam, and all sorts of other bases. In addition, their Better Than Gravy line will fool yo' grandmomma when you have to throw together gravy at the last second.

✓ The Food Saver vacuum sealer is an indispensable appliance in any kitchen. Its uses are myriad.

✓ When it comes to cooking whole chickens, nothing will improve the flavor and moisture content of the meat than proper brining.

✓ Almost every meat you cook will benefit from injections of a range of spices and appropriate fluids.

✓ The remote thermometer is a fine instrument to use when it comes to monitoring the internal temperature of larger cuts of meat.

✓ Remember to age your beef properly to enjoy its fullest potential of taste and tenderness.

✓ Concerning this matter of writing poems about food, especially recipes. It's like writing a poem about your wife—it almost cannot be done, because you can't do justice to it. What results from a recipe is far greater than the sum of its parts. (If you don't believe it, set the ingredients of my cornbread recipe before you and eat them before they become cornbread. See what I mean? Likewise, a poem and a wife are much greater than the sums of their parts.) As many essays as I've written about bacon and Spam, I cannot for the life of me write a poem about either one. Just won't work. Leave food to prose.

✓ Want to know what the best morning jump-start is? A big bowl of watermelon cubes. Mark Twain said that we know that the fruit Eve ate of in the Garden was not the Southern watermelon because she repented for taking it. That ain't it: God was still working on the watermelon, trying to make it the perfect fruit before introducing it. He succeeded.

from the desk of Jan Seale . . .

JUICY WRITING WITH FRUITS AND VEGGIES

Writing prompts:

1. fun with name of the f/v: "star fruit," "okra," "arugula," "collard"

2. favorite: to prepare; to eat

3. make a poem acrostic using name of fruit or vegetable

4. sensory description: "to let the tongue sing each fruit, its savor, its aroma, and its use." —Marge Piercy

5. celebration—"Slices, quarters, halves, or the whole hand holding an orange ball like the morning sun." —Mary Oliver

6. story behind: "I Cut Open a Papaya/My Husband Reads His UFO Journal" —Jan Seale

7. association: an orange as a toe bulge in Xmas stocking was "the best present"

8. saying: "She's not buying any green bananas." "No blood out of a turnip."

9. note/letter (implications): "I have eaten the plums that were in the icebox . . . ."   —W.C. Williams

10. metaphor: My life (soul) is like an apple (squash).

11. meditation on a scripture/reference/quote about fruit: "The fruit of the Spirit is love, joy, peace, patience, kindness, generosity, faithfulness, gentleness and self-control." Galatians 5:22 (New Testament, Bible)

HOW TO AVOID WRITER'S BLOCK IN POETRY

As I travelled the university/public school creative writing circuit during my reigning year as Texas Poet Laureate, I encountered a number of beginning poets who had experienced writer's block. Upon questioning these poets about their writing habits, it quickly became apparent to me that a large percentage of them, in seeking to compose the "Great American Poem" each time they sat down to write, had imposed ridiculous pressure on themselves and had forgotten the simple pleasure of playing with language, the phenomenon which steered them toward poetry in the first place. I suggested that they begin the writing process with play, for the sheer pleasure of it and it alone; jotting down on a page words which popped into their minds at random; crashing the words together like bumper cars just to see what happened. In doing this, they would notice that certain words might begin to coalesce into phrases in magical ways, phrases which, with a little luck, could be shaped into lines and stanzas. This play with language could also generate an image, completely unexpected; an image so startling that an entire first draft of a poem could be built around it. If the draft of a poem didn't develop during the exercise, the poet would at least have enjoyed the play with words this process would allow, and would not feel that the session was a total loss.

As Picasso is purported to have said, the magic of artistic creation comes to the grown-up artist who sees the world through the eyes of the child. And that is simply another way of relearning how to play.

Special Thanks . . .

... to Michael Ethredge ...

Thanks for all the ideas you nurtured, the patience you showed, and the guidance you gave your mom so that the project was a success.

...to Dr. Ruffin ...

Thanks for allowing each of us to find our own lessons to learn in editing and publishing this project. Especially, thanks for stepping out and letting us make this book full color.

... to Margaret Broussard ...

Thanks for giving us many Texas pictures to gain inspiration and creative ideas that brought this book to life.

... the Team ...

May this experience and the book we produced be a proud moment in our graduate studies. Thanks to everyone for lots of long hours and hard work. ee

The Team . . .

... Joanna Baker is a homeschooled high school graduate holding an AA from LSCS and a BA in English with honors from University of Houston-Downtown. She is   currently a graduate student in creative writing at SHSU.

... Matthew Bennett received his MA from SHSU in May of 2014. He has presented and published numerous essays, including his most recent work on Homer's epics and 1 Samuel. He currently lives in Spring, Texas.

... Reina Shay Broussard is a teacher, holistic health consultant, and writer seeking to empower others to their highest versions of themselves. She believes that changing your mind will change your life.

... Elizabeth Ethredge is a CIED graduate student minoring in English, wife to husband, James, for 33 years, and mother of two fantastic sons. She taught high school English for 9 years and is currently an adjunct professor at LoneStar College-University Park.

... Gary Horton is a retired geologist going back to college to learn how to write novels. He is presently well on his way toward an MFA in Creative Writing.

... Julian Kindred is a graduate student in English at SHSU and budding writer.